Rel. Life

OPEN TO THE SPIRIT
Religious Life after Vatican II

Open to the Spirit

RELIGIOUS LIFE AFTER VATICAN II

by

Ladislas M. Örsy, S.J.

CORPUS BOOKS
Washington—Cleveland

CORPUS PUBLICATIONS

Editorial Offices
1330 Massachusetts Ave., N.W.
Washington, D.C. 20005

Sales & Distribution
2231 West 110th Street
Cleveland, Ohio 44102

Library of Congress Catalog Card Number: 68-10453

First Printing, February 1968

Second Printing, August 1968

PRINTED IN THE UNITED STATES OF AMERICA

Preface

Pope John firmly believed that the Council he summoned would be the beginning of a new Pentecost for the Church. Indeed, the biblical signs of the coming of the Holy Spirit are all here and manifest: our houses are filled with a sound like the rush of a mighty wind, tongues of fire seem to appear in many places and the Good News is announced by many apostles with new courage in new languages.

The reactions of those watching these wondrous events are as varied today as they were on the day of the first Pentecost. Some are frightened by the wind and the tongues of fire (a deadly combination of elements!) and they cry danger. They forget that the Son of God came to set the earth on fire. Some are perplexed and confused by the new languages. They forget that Christ never promised to save his disciples from confusion, but that he promised them the light of his Spirit to guide them through it. Some are fearful and would like to keep the doors of the house locked. They forget that the kingdom of God is at hand, that the Scriptures are fulfilled, and the risen Lord has to be announced to the ends of the earth.

We all need the calm assurance of Peter: "In the days to come—it is the Lord who speaks—I will pour out my spirit on all mankind" (Acts 2, 17). These days to come are our days.

At the time of this new Pentecost the chapters of this book were born. Originally they were talks to religious communities of men and women in Rome, Canada, and the United States. They carry the mark of the time when they were conceived and given. They were intended to be communications of the word of God and some help in receiving the strength of the Holy Spirit in greater abundance. Although they are revised, the literary form of living speech is largely preserved in them; this causes some overlapping of ideas but it also witnesses to their gradual development. No one of the chapters is meant to be the final word on the matter; each is but one step in a dynamic movement towards a better understanding or deeper admiration of God's mystery in calling and consecrating his priests and prophets. Clearly other steps will have to follow.

No author is alone in producing his work: much of it is a personal expression of ideas assimilated in conversations and discussions with his friends. For such enrichment I am indebted principally to my fellow Jesuits: many lively debates with them preceded this book. In the preparation of the manuscript I was assisted by the Sisters of Saint Paul of Chartres in Rome: not even the Atlantic between us could diminish their readiness to help. Father Harold C. Gardiner, S.J., gave me firm support and brought his rich literary experience to the editing of the whole work. To them all I am grateful.

The first Pentecost was followed by the wonder of the diffusion of the Gospel and the expansion of the Church. If there is a new Pentecost today, we are witnessing only the beginnings of God's mighty deeds destined for our generations. To be open to the Spirit means to be ready to work new wonders with Christ today.

LADISLAS M. ÖRSY, S.J.

Assumption Day, 1967

ACKNOWLEDGMENTS

The chapters on Poverty and Chastity appeared originally in the *Review for Religious* (St. Marys, Kansas) in January 1967 and July 1967, respectively; the two chapters on Government in two special *Supplements* to *The Way* (London) in May 1966 and November 1967, respectively; each is republished here in somewhat revised form, with permission of the Editors.

Unless otherwise noted, quotations from Scripture are from *The Jerusalem Bible*, copyright © 1966 by Darton, Longman, & Todd, Ltd. and Doubleday & Company, Inc. Reprinted by permission of the publishers.

Unless otherwise stated, quotations from the Decrees of Vatican Council II are from *The Documents of Vatican II*, edited by Walter M. Abbott, S.J. (Herder and Herder, Association Press, New York; copyright 1966 by The America Press).

For the biblical background on Poverty I am greatly indebted to the work of Albert Gelin, *Les Pauvres de Yahve* (Paris, 1956).

For the biblical doctrine of Virginity I relied on some of the conclusions presented by Lucien Legrand, MEP, in his work, *The Biblical Doctrine of Virginity* (New York, 1963).

All through the preparation of the various chapters I made consistent use of the standard reference books for exegesis and biblical theology. The most important among them were: George A. Buttrick, ed., *The Interpreter's Dictionary of the Bible* (Nashville, 1962), Gerhard Kittel, ed., *Theologisches Wörterbuch zum neuen Testament* (Stuttgart, 1933, vol. 1.), Xavier Léon-Dufour, ed., *Vocabulaire de théologie biblique* (Paris, 1962), John McKenzie, *A Dictionary of the Bible* (Milwaukee, 1965), Alan Richardson, ed., *Theological Word Book of the Bible,* (New York, 1962).

Contents

1

Prophets of the New Covenant

Consecrated religious life is a living fact in the Church. It developed in the earliest centuries, and has existed ever since. It rejoiced in periods of splendor, and it suffered the bitter experience of decline—yet it never died. After each crisis, it recovered and manifested signs of internal strength. It showed also a remarkable capacity to adapt to the needs of every age; it was continually enriched with new, external forms. Only its sudden total demise would reveal the extent of the involvement of consecrated religious persons in the life and the work of the Church: schools, hospitals, radio stations, orphanages, and leprosaria would be abandoned, and the children of God left crying for bread and dying from hunger.

Religious life is a living fact. It proceeds not so much from any human planning as from the action of the Spirit. As with all things that come from the Spirit, we first experience it, and then try to reflect on it and to translate the riches of God's gift into human terms.

The aim of these reflections is precisely to express in human terms some of the divine riches that are revealed in the life of consecrated communities. It will be an effort that can be crowned by partial success only; we can never express adequately what is contained in God's gift. But the prospect of inadequacy is not a justification for remaining silent. Any attempt to reveal God's mystery to man is worth the effort.

THE PLACE OF RELIGIOUS IN THE CHURCH: WHAT IS THE PROBLEM?

In the years immediately preceding Vatican Council II, a debate arose among theologians concerning the place of religious life in the Church. With some injustice to carefully qualified theological positions, the terms of the debate can be summed up by the following question: is religious life part of the structure of the Church, or is it a movement within the structure of the Church?

To be part of the structure of the Church, or to belong to the essential structure of the Church meant, in the debaters' terms, a permanent quality, a stability by divine institution and divine guarantee. The episcopal hierarchy is an essential part of the structure of the Church; it is of divine origin; no man can abolish it. If religious life belongs to the structure of the Church, its existence cannot be touched by man, and, like the episcopate, it will endure to the end of time.

To be a movement within the framework of the essential structure of the Church means that religious life has a fragile quality. Even though it may flourish, its existence would not have a divine origin, nor its survival a divine guarantee; the Church could well live without it. If any judgment is formed about the need for religious life, it should be in the terms of natural and supernatural expediency. Religious life would be essentially under the power of human law. Popes and bishops would have full freedom, legally and morally, to bless religious communities or to suppress them, without fear that they would be interfering with the essential structure of the Church.

The terms in which the debate is here reported may be unjustly concise, but they help to state the problem clearly: what is the place of religious life in the Church? Can consecrated religious persons claim that their way of life is of divine institution, or should they humbly admit that it is an all-too-human phenomenon in the Church, subject not only to reform or renewal, but to radical reconsideration to the point of allowing its disappearance?

The answer here attempted may be summed up by saying: consecrated religious life is the *existential* gift of God to his Church, a special fruit of the dynamic action of the Holy Spirit in the Church. This short answer needs a long explanation, but before beginning the explanation, it will help us to reflect on God's personal qualities; on God as he is and as he has revealed himself to us. A better knowledge of the giver leads to a deeper understanding of the gift.

Should we not say that sometimes we pay lip service to an all-powerful God, source of all beauty, and then, in practice, reduce his image to our own small measure? Should we not admit that, in the Church, God has been frequently presented to the faithful as the God of order and discipline, and very rarely as the God of beauty and spontaneous artistry? Such misrepresentations have undoubtedly occurred. We all know how legal considerations have reigned supreme in our daily Christian life, how we have insisted on immutable structures, and how little attention we have paid to the fact that God created poetry, art, and music—which cannot be subject to any stern legalistic discipline.

Certainly, God is the God of order and immutable foundations, but he is, as well, the God of artistic disorder and lively change. No institution on the face of the earth, be it human or divine, can ever reflect the full image of God, unless it reflects both God's love of order and precision and his freedom in the creation of surprising beauty.

Among all institutions on the earth the most divine is the Church. God made it to his own image, and the Church must reflect that image to the end of time. There will be strong order and precise foundations in the Church, and there will be, also, the surprising creative freedom of the Spirit.

HIERARCHY AND PROPHECY

Peter was called to be the rock on which the Church was built. Into that rock the apostles, living stones, were incorporated, so that with Peter they could form one foundation, the apostolic college. Their power was, and still is, handed down from generation to generation through a sacramental rite. It is a power that has its source in God; no human limitation or sinfulness can destroy it. As the apostles formed a college, so do the bishops—the pope taking the place of Peter.

The episcopal college belongs to the essential structure of the Church; the people of God cannot live without their shepherds. The shepherds alone do not constitute the Church—the whole people of God are the Church—but the shepherds bring stability into the life of the Church; they are the trustees of Christ's doctrine, and they have the power to feed and to lead the flock of the Master. Their main function is divinely defined and guaranteed; they cannot lose the word of God and they cannot lead God's people in a substantially wrong direction.

The hierarchical structure in the Church represents God's stability, the permanence of his Word, and the firmness of his love, but this is not the full image of God. The Church must also reflect and reveal the surprising and creative freedom of God. This part of God's image cannot be so evident in the permanent structures; to us they appear unchangeable. The God of surprising love, of creative art, and of all that is poetry and music is more clearly revealed by the immediate inspiration that he imparts to some of his friends, to some of his chosen ones. If the institution of the papacy reveals the strength of God's love, the inspiration of St. Francis of Assisi tells us that the same love is filled with romance and poetry.

Religious life is mainly the fruit of the free and dynamic action of the Spirit in the Church; it is an existential gift from God to the Church, through which God wants to reveal the ever fresh, ever surprising beauty of his love. Although God did not make religious life part of the divine structure of the Church, that life is not merely the invention of devoted and holy men. It is the fruit of the action of the Spirit in the Church; through it God reveals himself in a special way. He manifests his presence in the Church with the freedom of an artist and a poet, giving new inspirations to chosen persons, bringing to life new communities with new forms.

The prototype of God's free, existential gift to the Church is the virgin from Nazareth, Mary. She had no share in the power of Peter; did not fill the office of an apostle. She had to move the Church by inspiration, and not by any external power, and yet, can the impact of her personality on the Church ever be measured? She is the prototype of the religious vocation; she received a gift that did not originate in any external structure, yet she received a spiritual mission from God. It was a mission to inspire, not a mission to govern or to rule. Consecrated religious are given a similar type of vocation: to be enriched by the Spirit and to be a source of pure spiritual inspiration to the Church. In this sense, the vocation to consecrated religious life is an existential gift of God to the Church. God gives his inspiration with supreme freedom to individual persons and to communities, in view of various needs and necessities in the Church. His inspiration takes place within the structure of the Church, but its fruit does not become part of the essential structure. It reflects the free creative power of God. Religious life is therefore a gift from the Spirit. The Church, consequently, has the duty to accept this divine gift, to protect and foster it.

THE PROPHETS OF THE NEW COVENANT

With some justification and legitimate simplification it is possible to say that in the life of the Hebrew nation, the chosen people of God in the Old Testament, there were two main balancing factors: the institution of a kingdom, and prophetic inspiration—in concrete terms, the kings and the prophets.

The kings represented a unifying force, an external power. In spite of the shortcomings of the monarchy and its rulers, the twelve tribes of Israel were united by the institution of a kingdom, and from it the foundations for future political structures, necessary for the existence of a nation, were laid.

The other source of vitality for the Israelites was the prophetic movement. The prophets did not have, as a rule, any external power, and they did not represent any strong structure. Their strength was spiritual; it lay in the word of God that was given to them from above. Their vocation was to announce the word to all the children of Israel—a purely spiritual mission. Without the prophets, the external political structure of the tribes of Israel would have been an empty framework; with them it was filled with a deep spiritual meaning.

Without stressing the analogy too far, it is possible to discern that there are similar balancing factors in the life of the Church, God's people of the New Covenant. There is the strong external structure, represented by Peter and the apostles, and a prophetic inspiration, represented primarily by the Virgin Mary. Peter and the apostles handed down their power to the bishops, who form the episcopal college with the pope as their head. The Holy Spirit inspired a number of men and women to follow the type of life that the Virgin Mary led, in virginity and poverty. Both are necessary for the Church: external organization and spiritual inspiration.

To avoid any misunderstanding, let us say clearly that these two balancing factors manifest two types of power, which can be analytically discerned and notionally distinguished in the Church. But the two powers may, and in fact often do, come together in the same person who has both the power to govern and the capacity to inspire. This is always the ideal situation, but the two powers can exist separately too, a less-than-ideal situation. Yet it is important to maintain, as an essential of Catholic doctrine, that the validity of the possession of the power to govern in the

Church does not depend on the personal capacity to inspire. The power to rule is always there, even if the ruler reveals no personal inspiration; God assists him because of his office. But, let us repeat, the ideal situation is that the rulers should also be prophets. In that case the two main balancing factors will become one in the same person, as they were one in the person of Peter and the apostles.

When the existing realities of the Church are subject to a theological analysis, however, we have to say that personal prophetic inspiration is not of the essence of government. If that were so, we should respect and obey the commands of our bishops only when their inspiration is proved—which is not the doctrine of our faith. But we must say that prophetic inspiration is of the essence of the emergence and permanence of religious life in the Church; without it, religious life simply could not come into being, still less endure.

Although the ideal situation is that the rulers should be prophets, it is not always the ideal situation that the prophets should be rulers too. It is a fair rule that religious should have no ambition to govern; not because an office or dignity in the Church is not good or holy, but simply because religious have a different vocation, which is to manifest to all in the Church the ever fresh, surprising, creative activity of the Spirit. It is by remaining what they are that they make the greatest contribution to the life of the Church and offer the most effective help to its shepherds, the bishops. This was realized by many founders of religious institutes who consistently refused to allow the members to accept an ecclesiastical office or dignity. In no way did they consider that to be a shepherd of the flock was not an exalted vocation; their respect for bishops should refute any such accusation. But they knew that their vocation was a different one: it was the vocation to inspire the people of God.

In this age of the New Covenant, religious have a prophetic vocation—and nothing else. (The term prophet is used here in the biblical sense, and not in the sense that modern English gives to it. In the biblical sense, a prophet is a person who has a personal spiritual mission, that is, to be a witness to the strength of God, to the love of God for his people. In modern English prophet means a person who foretells the future. Religious have no such privilege or gift, and let us hope that God will never give it to them.) This is not to say that there are not other prophets; there are. This is not to say that other vocations are not holy; they are. It is simply to state that the purity of religious vocation consists in the purity of prophecy, by words, by deeds, and by daily life.

To be a prophet means to be a witness, or to be a sign. A witness tells about a fact he knows from personal experience. Therefore his words have a special freshness, they ring convincingly, they arouse assent. A religious is a living witness of the presence and of the creative action of the Spirit in the Church; it is the Spirit who called him to his vocation. A sign is something that connects persons, or connects a person with an object. A sign leads a person somewhere: to a place, to an object, or to another person. Religious, by their life, connect this world with God's eternity; they are a sign to all that there is an eternal kingdom of God.

CHARISMATIC LIFE

Religious life is also called a charismatic way of life. This is a correct way of referring to it: the life of the prophets *is* a

charismatic way of life. It will therefore help us to understand religious life better if we try to explain what is
meant in the traditional language of the Church by
charism and the charismatic way of life.

Charism in general means a spiritual gift from God, a
gift of the Holy Spirit. Those gifts can be of a large variety; St. Paul enumerates many of them:

> There is a variety of gifts but always the same Spirit . . .
> the gift of preaching with wisdom . . . the gift of preach-
> ing instruction . . . the gift of faith . . . the gift of healing
> . . . the power of miracles . . . prophecy . . . the gift of
> recognising spirits . . . the gift of tongues and . . . the
> ability to interpret them. All these are the work of one
> and the same Spirit, who distributes different gifts to
> different people just as he chooses (1 Cor 12, 4–11).

Among these gifts, the three theological virtues are
included: ". . . There are three things that last: faith, hope
and love; and the greatest of these is love" (1 Cor 13, 13).
Charism in a general sense, therefore, means any spiritual
gift, including the greatest, which is love.

Charism, in a more particular sense, means a spiritual
gift that is not identical with any of the theological virtues.
Even such a charism, however, would have a close relationship to charity; for every gift has its roots in charity and
therefore disposes us to grow in charity and love.

When we speak about the charism of religious vocation, or about the charismatic way of life of religious persons and communities, we do not mean, specifically, the
charism of charity; rather, we mean other spiritual gifts
that have their origin in charity, and also help charity to
grow and develop. This must be so, because if the charisms
given to those who have a religious vocation are identical

with charity, then every Christian would have a vocation to be a religious, which is certainly not true. Therefore, the charisms of religious cannot be identical with divine charity, but will be something that grows out of charity and helps it to increase.

The charismatic gifts of the Holy Spirit are always given to persons. They are instrumental in deepening the personal relationship between God and man. They have another effect too: they influence the human personality of the one who receives them. It would be enough to recall, in this context, the charisms of preaching, of counseling, of being an apostle. These gifts have an impact on the human person and give him new riches; they help him to reach fuller maturity.

Some charisms can be said to be given for the sake of a community, but this is simply a way of speaking; all gifts of the Holy Spirit are given to persons since God speaks as person to person. But God can give similar gifts to many persons, and when those who receive similar or identical gifts gather together and form a community, then the common gift will produce a common spirit and a common dedication. In such a case we can speak properly about a charismatic community. Further, by their very union among themselves, their gifts acquire a new strength; a communion comes into being based on the sharing of similar or identical gifts.

Religious life, moreover, is marked by specific charisms. They are usually designated by the terms chastity, poverty, and obedience. This terminology is traditional, and expresses the truth reasonably well, but it is possible to find better terms and better descriptions of the charisms that God offers to those who are called to religious life.

God offers them the gift of his own companionship, which is so absorbing that the person so favored wants to vow chastity. He offers them the possession of the earth, which is so enriching that the person wants to be free from particular possessions and hence vows poverty. He offers them a close incorporation into the visible church through an ecclesial community (which is the religious community), in order to continue the saving acts of Christ, his preaching, his care for the sick, his love for God's little ones. The acceptance of this last offer is expressed by the vow of obedience. It is not usual to describe the charisms of religious life in this way; but the terms chastity, poverty, and obedience describe more exactly the consequences of God's invisible gifts in a visible world than the full reality. Let us note again that God's invisible gifts given to religious blossom out of faith, hope, and charity, but are not identical with these theological virtues.

This explanation of the meaning of charism and charismatic life is admittedly not exhaustive. It should be enough to state clearly that within the context of this essay the term charism means a spiritual gift and the charisms of religious life the specific spiritual gifts of consecrated religious persons and communities: the companionship of God, the possession of the earth, the close incorporation into the visible structure of the Church in order to continue the saving acts of Christ. Not one of these special charisms is identical with divine charity, but all of them are closely related to it. They have value and meaning only insofar as they spring from charity and help to preserve and increase it. Charity is the best gift that God can give, and it is given to all Christians.

THE CHARISM OF VIRGINITY:
THE GIFT OF GOD'S
COMPANIONSHIP

The foundation of religious vocation is a special gift of God by which he offers to some chosen persons his companionship in a special way all through their life. This offer of God contains a promise of friendship, a promise of God's particular presence with them—a presence that will lead them, comfort them, and strengthen them. This companionship or friendship means an experiential union with God that is designed to be so strong as to exclude companionship with another human being in the sacrament of marriage. The promise of this union through the gentle inspiration of the Holy Spirit, or the union itself, has for its effect the consecration of the person in virginity. Virginity is not the union; it is rather the fruit of union and at the same time its protection. Virginity should be understood as a spiritual virtue and value that is instilled at the moment of this total, life-long dedication to God. Consecrated virginity cannot be temporal; to manifest the fullness of giving, it has to be perpetual.

When God offers his special friendship to a human person, he effectively promises to fill the person's mind with grace and light in such a way that the emptiness left by the absence of a human companion will be filled by the abundance of God's gifts. God also promises so to strengthen even the body that the sense of frustration that the lack of human companionship induces will be counterweighed by his love and power. Precisely because God promises grace and light to the mind, consecrated virginity is the best disposition for the development of a life of prayer and contemplation. Moreover, because God promises his strength, virginity is the best beginning of a life of practical charity.

This gift of God is a charism of permanent friendship and companionship. God could, no doubt, give temporal gifts of many kinds, but the charism of consecrated friendship, from which virginity flows, is perpetual. It is to last until death and beyond. Perpetual virginity follows from the offer of companionship precisely because God, in his greatness and generosity, offers a lasting gift, for the whole life of a man. It is a spiritual gift; it is not a substitute for naturally good things. It does not fulfill a natural need; it gives strength to live happily in a new way. The lack of human fulfillment is balanced by divine power.

It is clear, then, why neither of the two terms, perfect chastity or virginity, describes the essence of the first charism in consecrated religious life. The first charism is God's special friendship, his companionship, his uninterrupted conversation with the person all through a human life, his unceasing strength that sustains the person in all difficulties. The one who receives the gift of this friendship and companionship does not want to marry; he does not want to share his mind, his heart, and his body with another human person, because human nature is too limited for two overwhelming relationships. When there is a genuine vocation to consecrated life, God fills the heart of a man so completely that he does not desire to take a human companion. It does not follow that a consecrated person will be cold toward his fellow men; his charity will overflow to everyone, but will not be exclusively concentrated on any one.

To try to describe in theological terms this charism of God's companionship within the framework of consecrated virginity is a challenging task, but it is, nevertheless, possible. The charism is an anticipation of the great grace of resurrection; it is a small, but significant, irruption of the grace of immortality into a mortal human being. It may seem surprising to describe thus this gift of God's friendship in virginity, but there is no doubt that those who are celibates or virgins "for the sake of the kingdom" receive a new light and strength that keep them whole and in balance, and turned towards God in spite of the natural inclination and attraction towards marriage. This balance is beyond any human strength; it cannot come from anyone other than the Holy Spirit. It brings a new life, and only the Spirit of God can give new life in our new creation. He gave life to the humanity of Christ through the Virgin Mary, and new life to the dead body of Christ. Now it is the same Holy Spirit, giver of life, who takes possession of a human person and gives him strength to lead a life that is an anticipation of the life of eternity in its unique and exclusive relationship with God.

From this special friendship with God, there follows a special mission in the Church. Consecrated virgins, more than anyone else, declare the absolute value of God's friendship and the absolute value of eternal life. They bypass the good (and it is a great good) of marriage, and they assume, with their consecration, the way of life of those who are in God's eternity.

This special friendship with God is independent of the external structures of the Church. It is given by the Holy Spirit to those whom he chooses according to his own will. It is the fruit of a person-to-person relationship between the Holy Spirit and a person. When someone is called to religious life, this is the first gift he receives; in fact, this is probably the greatest and most fundamental gift. Through it God gives his presence and his strength, and his gift has an effect on the whole person—on mind, heart, and even body. There are few graces which are so far-reaching. No wonder, then, that the sacrifice asked for in exchange by God is also great. Man has to offer his intelligence, his will power, and even his body to God.

Virginity sets a person apart in the Church. It makes him somewhat different from others, perhaps even secluded, but not for long. There is a dynamic movement in the gift of virginity, or better, in the gift of this friendship with God. This movement begins by the person turning to God and away from the world. It continues when the consecrated celibate or virgin, after having learned more about God's personal love for man, comes back to the world in order to bring God's blessings to it. He becomes an instrument of grace. Yet let us keep in mind that virginity is not identical with charity. It is a framework for the development of charity, source and fruit of love at the same time.

THE CHARISM OF POVERTY: THE GIFT OF THE POSSESSION OF THE EARTH

Virginity is a special, concrete fruit of God's dynamic love for a person. Another such fruit of the same love is poverty. Virginity frees a person from close personal ties; poverty frees him from ties to material wealth. Poverty does not have the same meaning in modern English that it has in ecclesiastical language. In modern English, poverty means primarily impoverishment and misery, in ecclesiastical language it means both detachment from, and the dedicated use of, material things. It means an internal freedom from slavery to things, and also the use of things with moderation and discretion for the sake of God's kingdom. This difference in meanings causes a great deal of confusion; at times it gives rise to the accusation of hypocrisy. In English, poverty has a material, and only a material, connotation; in religious language, poverty has a spiritual and primarily a spiritual meaning. Admittedly, spiritual poverty must have a material expression; the internal must be manifested externally, but the external manifestation of spiritual poverty may lie in frugality, simplicity, and discretion, and not in impoverishment. In ordinary English, poverty is incompatible with extensive use of material things; in religious language, poverty may even, and generally does, postulate the use of created things for the sake of the kingdom. Perhaps it would be better if we did not speak so much about poverty, but rather about the dedicated use of created things in a Christ-like way.

Poverty, like virginity, is a fruit of God's special friendship. Behind the mere absence of riches, a rich, positive charism is operative. This positive gift of God is not easy to define, but it can be called the gift of the possession of the earth. This possession is not material or legal, but rather spiritual, possible for those who are free interiorly. They can then take possession of the whole world and make it serve God, in accordance with his plan as it is made known to them. Obviously no other person can enjoy this spiritual possession of the earth than he who is free from attachment to particular things, that is, who is free to receive and free to give. Poverty means both the capacity to receive and to give.

God's poor ones have the capacity to receive all the gifts that either God, or a human person, or inanimate creation itself offers them. They are open and empty to receive graces from God, ideas and suggestions from other persons, and beauty that delights and refreshes the mind and heart from nature itself. God's poor ones have also the capacity to give. Only a poor person is free enough to give away what he has. He is ready to give to others his material wealth; he is willing to put his intelligence at the service of his neighbor, and above all, he is disposed to give away his own person. He desires to become the property of Christ, ready to serve whenever there is a need.

Poverty, therefore, means the capacity to give. In order to be introduced into spiritual freedom it is necessary to give up material things. Then the giving away of intellectual possessions—our own ideas and plans—should follow. But the highest and the most exquisite manifestation of religious poverty is the giving away of our own person for the sake of our neighbor, for the sake of our fellow man, especially the spiritually and materially poor. Poverty means to give ourselves away so that all men can use us as a help, as a guide to God. That is the most that a poor person can give. It is not an irrational giving; it is for the sake of the kingdom. It is not a dispersal of our best forces, but a concentration on one purpose—the expansion of the kingdom. Into this expansion the poor man throws his whole personality—mind, heart, and body—so that he can be used by the Church and by his fellow men to reach God and help them reach God. One poor person gives himself to others who are poor, to help them find the riches of God.

Another manifestation of poverty of heart is the acceptance of a life in which all security comes from the presence of the Spirit, and not through any other means. The real impediment to progress in spiritual poverty for religious often lurks in their love of earthly security, and in their flight from the insecurity of the Spirit. To acquire earthly security is one of the strongest human instincts, and the greatest of the rich man's luxuries. A rich man seeks security through the acquisition of large estates, through good investments, through buying stocks and bonds. The security they promise often leads him to rely on them and not on God, and consequently God's providence does not enter his life as an effective force.

Religious, too, can build up earthly security through estates, investments, stocks and bonds (all property of the community, of course), but more frequently, religious seek for themselves an earthly security by spiritual means: through laws, rules, customs, and regulations. Such laws are conceived with a view to any eventuality that may arise, so that whenever a new challenge comes from God's providence, there is a standing legal provision to handle it, although the challenge would have required a new departure, a new inspiration. Security is established through subtle intellectual and spiritual means; its effect, however, can be as deadly as when it is done by material means. Religious lose their mobility and flexibility, their capacity to give fresh answers to God's new challenges. When in difficulties, they rely on man-made structures and not on the assistance of the Spirit. Every crisis is solved by casuistry, not by creative inspiration.

These observations do not aim to destroy those rules and regulations, but to state their real value. Christ did not promise any external or material security to his disciples. He did not tell them beforehand how, exactly, they should answer the challenge of oppressive emperors and pagan philosophers. He did not give them security by preset and detailed rules; he gave them assurance by promising his strengthening presence and the sending of his

Spirit. Christ established his apostles in an earthly insecurity and a heavenly security. The key factor in this heavenly security was their faith in God's providence. Religious
can destroy this fine balance between earth and heaven
and shift the weight of their life to earth by establishing a
perfect system in which everything is foreseen and provided for, and there is no room any more for the refreshing
providence of God. God himself may send them a personal
challenge that asks for a creative response, but to no avail,
for the divine initiative may merely end up as one more
legal case to be disposed of by "competent authority."

Poverty of heart means freedom from slavery to laws,
rules, and regulations in order to be able to move with the
Holy Spirit. It does not mean that there should be no laws
and rules; they are as necessary to a community as are
bones to a human body, but bones should not take the
place of flesh and blood. Similarly, laws should be kept in
right proportion; they should be a base for new depar-
tures, and not a prison from which there are no depar-
tures.

There is a parallelism between virginity and poverty.
Each is the fruit of God's dynamic action in a human person. In offering the gift of his companionship, God draws a
person away from a human relationship, in order to enrich
him in his divine friendship, and to make him a source of
grace for many. In offering a person the possession of the
earth, God draws him away from particular attachments to
created possessions, be they material or spiritual, in order
to enrich him with a general mission to sanctify this created world. A consequence of God's friendship is virginity;
a further consequence is poverty, or freedom with regard
to possessions. Both virginity and poverty are personal

charisms. They are not necessarily connected with the external structure of the Church; they can be practiced outside of any religious community; that is to say, they can exist legitimately in individual persons without the hierarchy of the Church being notified of God's graces. Virginity is the first, and most fundamental, of these gifts because there precisely this close personal relationship with God is established; there precisely a man opens up to God. The gift of the possession of the earth follows; God gives his creation to the one whom he made his personal friend. This gift, too, develops through a dialectic movement. The person called to possess the whole of creation in general, but nothing in particular, will go through a period of enforced deprivation—an experience of the desert, in order to free himself from slavish attachments. This will be followed by a period of rest in God's riches. Finally, he will come back to the world free and enriched to build the kingdom of God with all available spiritual and material means.

THE CHARISM OF OBEDIENCE: THE GIFT OF DEDICATION TO CHRIST IN AN ECCLESIAL COMMUNITY

Whenever the Holy Spirit imparts his special gifts, he likes to draw the recipient closer to the visible Church—to the Church that is the living Christ on earth. Although it is quite possible that one who enjoys the gifts of virginity and poverty may remain unknown to the Church, in most of the cases the friends of God will look towards the visible Church; and will ask for a closer, more visible connection with her. They will frequently offer themselves to share the work of the Church.

The freedom that arises from virginity and poverty

enables a person to have a better vision of the Church, of its divine and human qualities. He will discern more clearly the presence of the word of God in the visible Church, and he will have the capacity to experience more vividly the invisible action of the Spirit in the visible Christian community. He will recognize the presence of Christ in the episcopal college, for he will see the divine qualities in the Church through human representatives. The sign of divine inspiration lies precisely in seeing the two together: the divine qualities and the human limitations, to believe in what is divine without being shocked by what is human, such as the shortcomings, and even the sins of Christians—sins that somehow soil the Church herself. A charismatic person will be attracted to the Church, visible and invisible, because all charisms are from the Spirit, and the Church's soul is the Spirit. All charisms are given for the sanctification of men, and in the Church lives Christ who came to redeem and sanctify all men. All charisms lead to Christ: here on earth the Church is Christ.

When one who possesses the gifts of virginity and poverty offers himself to do the specific work of the Church, he desires a closer incorporation into the visible structure of the Church—an incorporation that represents a closer union with Christ. He wants to enter into a covenant with Christ made present among us through the Church. Within the structure of the Church, he wants to be a member of an ecclesial community so that in and with the Church he can continue the saving acts of Christ. Normally, therefore, the gifts of virginity and poverty will be followed by the gift of dedication to the specific work of the Church in an ecclesial community, and from this dedication the grace of obedience arises.

Here we have to pause to understand what the specific work of the Church is. St. Paul stresses the strong identity of the Church with Christ. The specific work of the Church, consequently, must be substantially identical with the work of Christ; in other words, with the mission of Christ, the commission Christ received from his Father. Christ was sent to reveal God's mystery to us, to preach the good news, to forgive the sinner, to heal the sick, to give sight to the blind, and to comfort the poor. The mission of the Church is the same, a spiritual mission: to continue the saving acts of Christ, to bring the message of the Father to all men, to pray for the remission of all sins, to preach the good news, to heal the sick (more in a spiritual than a material sense), and to comfort the poor. Any community that exists within the Church, and above all a religious community that has been approved, blessed, and fostered by the Church, serves the same purpose. The purpose of the mission of Christ, of the Church, and of religious communities within the Church is the same: the salvation and sanctification of men.

It follows that when a person, virgin and poor, asks for a closer incorporation into the visible Church, he is really asking, in the Spirit, to take up the specific work of Christ, and to continue the actions of Christ. All religious communities have an ecclesial character, for Christ lives in them as he lives in the Church: he lives in the parts as he lives in the whole. He is the source of life in a religious community as he is the source of life in the Church. One who gives himself to the Church in a community is repeating the gesture of the apostles who left their nets and followed Christ—closer than anyone else. This consideration is of capital importance for the understanding of the charism of dedicated, or consecrated, life in an ecclesial community.

FURTHER CLARIFICATION OF THE CHARISM OF OBEDIENCE: A RELIGIOUS COMMUNITY IS AN ORGANIC BODY

We come now to the consideration of a religious community. To understand its meaning and purpose, its internal and external structure, it will help to consider how a religious community comes into being, how it is built up, and finally, what its place is in the Church.

The beginning of a religious community, historically, is in the act of the first members who, having received the same graces and gifts from God, gather together and offer themselves to the Church in order to continue the work of Christ in the Church. When the Church accepts their offer and officially sanctions their way of life, the mystery of the incarnation is fulfilled in the life of a probably small pioneering group. The internal graces bear fruit in an external structure; the inspiration given by the Spirit is recognized by the Church, the living Christ on earth. From this union of the internal graces and the external seal, a new cell, a new organ in the mystical body of Christ arises. A new religious community is born.

The essential element in all religious communities, old and new, is the union of minds and hearts, the identical charisms that all members share, and the common purpose that the community pursues. This internal element is what shapes a loose group of persons into a community. Beyond any difference in space and time, it binds together different individuals who are occupied in various works, but have the same mind and heart, the same purpose. This internal union is the soul of a community, but a soul that must be embodied; the internal unity, therefore, requires an external expression. The external expression may be manifold and varied. It may consist in "common life" in a strict sense, as when religious follow the same order of the day, and wear the same habit. It may consist in regular meetings, in team work without strict external uniformity, in common planning and execution of work—without all the traditional elements of "common life." The essential is the internal unity; the soul is the source of life in a community. The accidental element is the external togetherness which, to some extent, is necessary but which, in itself, does not make a group into community. When we speak about the "common life" of religious, we should primarily intend this common mind and heart, and not uniformity in timetables and daily life.

The proper definition of a religious community in the Church should be "a community of consecrated persons who have received a mission in the Church to continue the saving acts of Christ." This is a theological definition which, as yet, has not been translated into the terms of canon law. A religious community should be defined by its common mission in the Church, from which "common life" will follow whenever it is good for the mission, and not follow when it impedes the purpose of the mission. This definition does justice to both monasteries of monks and to religious communities working in far-spread mission areas. Both types of communities are one internally, but the monks express their unity by living together according to a fairly uniform pattern; missionary religious express their unity by periodical meetings, correspondence, and dependence on each other in counseling and government.

When a religious community is officially approved

and formed, it takes its place in the Church. Clearly, its essential aim and purpose cannot be anything else than that of the Church, which is to continue the saving acts of Christ, and this essentially religious purpose will have to penetrate into every single member of the community and inspire all individual and collective actions.

The internal structure of a religious community is marked by a basic equality and accidental differences. The equality springs from the union of each of the members with the Holy Spirit; everyone in the community is a temple of the Holy Spirit. Moreover, everyone received the same charism to serve God in this community according to the spirit of this institute. Apart from the common, Christian vocation, they all share a particular vocation manifested through a particular charism. They all are virgins, poor, and they all are dedicated to the aims of their institute. There is, accordingly, a double source of equality —every member is a child of God, and every menber is chosen for the same particular vocation in this community.

The differences in the community originate in the diversity of God's graces and gifts, natural or supernatural. The differences, however, are accidental. Moreover, some differences can originate in the various functions that the members exercise in the community—one is called to pray, another to preach, a third to heal, another to be the shepherd of the rest of the flock. These are all functions in the external life of the community. They establish a certain hierarchy in the organization of daily life and the community's work; but since they are external functions, they can never touch the basic unity and equality in God's love and in the common charism of the institute.

The internal and invisible structure of the institute is

marked by the intensity of charity in each of the members, known to God alone. The external and visible structure of the institute is marked by various functions which, in themselves, do not necessarily increase charity; they should, accordingly, never be exalted above charity. In fact, it should be constantly brought home to all the members that the best of all charisms is charity.

The external structure is marked by various relationships. General mutual relationships exist among all the members, but there are also particular relationships between the head and each individual member. The relationships among members are sources of rights and duties within the community. Each member has the right to be understood, helped, and respected by the others as a human person and a child of God, and all have the duty to give what these rights postulate. The relationships between the head and each individual member are the foundation for authority and obedience, with a complex set of rights and duties on both sides. In fact, the authority and obedience relationship is best understood if we consider it in the context of dedication to God and to the Church in an ecclesial community, a community that is continuing the saving work of Christ.

The best and most evangelical description of those in authority is that they are the shepherds of the flock. They are not, however, shepherds in their own right; they have to feed and to lead the flock in the name of Christ who is the Good Shepherd. They are trustees; they govern in the name of another. The style of government they have to exercise can best be described as a loving care of their flock. A theological qualification of the concept of shepherd-and-flock is, however, necessary. In reality there is no equality between a shepherd and his flock; in a religious community there is equality. Although there is a fundamental difference between the Good Shepherd and the flock, since he is divine, there is no substantial difference between the head and the members of the flock in a purely human community. We speak about the shepherd and the flock, but *all* have the same human nature, and *all* share the same divine nature and the same charismatic gifts.

The mission of the shepherd (superior) in a community is the same as the mission of the flock (the community) : to continue the saving work of Christ in the Church. Those in authority receive their power for this end, and for no other. The source of the specifically religious power of the superior is the Church. The Church commissions him to be the head of the community, and to take loving care of all the members. He governs those who are in equal possession of the essential gifts of God. There is, however, another source of power for the superior: the fact that there is a community. This source is human; the power arises from a human fact, and not from a specifically religious purpose. It gives the right to bring reasonable order into the life of the community. A wise superior will use it with great restraint, just so far as it is necessary for the main religious purpose.

The relationships that arise among all the members can best be described as diversity in unity, since there is an accidental diversity among the members in supernatural and natural gifts, and an essential unity in the same. Good community life never means perfect uniformity; rather it means perfect respect for reality by honoring this diversity in unity. Greater sacrifice and greater dedication are probably required to admit differences, honor them, and let them develop than to try to reduce everything to a monot-

perpetual vows. Like any other virtue, this life and work in a community under one head is subject to development; it does not reach its perfection in the beginning, and it requires flexibility and suppleness. It reaches its perfection, not when all the acts of a person are dictated from above, but when the right balance for a community or a type of work is reached between the direction of the superior and creative contribution on the part of the members.

AUTHORITY IS ESSENTIAL IN RELIGIOUS LIFE: IT CAN BE CORPORATE OR PERSONAL

At present, there cannot be a religious community in the Church unless there is an authority in that community. A loose group in which there is no authority, in which all decisions are taken by common deliberations, and whose decisions do not bind the members of the community, would not be admitted as a religious community within the present legal structure of the Church.

This is not to say that there is no room in the Church for consecrated persons who want to live together in a loose group without in any way tying themselves to the community through the relationship of authority and obedience, but it is to say that they would not be accepted today as a religious community. They could have a specific charism to live in a community without any authority, but this would not be the specific charism of religious life, since dedication in an organic community seems to belong to the essence of religious life. Whether this is a theological necessity, or a mere question of discipline, is difficult to decide. In all probability, the foundation for it is theological because, by living in an organic, structured commu-

nity, one is more fully incorporated into the visible
Church. If there is a possibility for the members of a group
of consecrated persons to leave the community at any time
or to dissent from it in everything, dedication to the specific work of the Church does not fully exist; the visible
bond with the visible Church remains loose. Therefore,
the covenant between the living Christ, that is, the
Church, and the members of the group, does not exist.
Such unstructured groups do not have the same status and,
theologically, cannot have the same status in the Church as
the groups that have an organic structure.

This organic structure implies authority. Although
there are many theological distinctions concerning authority, here the term means jurisdiction, and what is known
as dominative or domestic power. It is certain that, in a
duly approved and constituted religious community, a
power is given by the Church to those who govern, a power
that does not arise only from the consent of the members.
The structure of power may vary according to the constitutions of the institute. It is different in an exempt clerical institute, or in a lay institute of pontifical right, or of diocesan right.

The source of religious authority is the Church.
Jurisdiction in the strict sense is the communication of the
episcopal power. In the case of so-called dominative or
domestic power, the right to govern arises from the mandate of the Church, from the fact that the Church entrusts
a work to a particular community. From the mandate the
necessity of an organic life arises; without authority no
community can exist for long. It follows that all superiors
have, somehow, a power given to them by the Church.
This seems certain on theological grounds.

Apart from the power that comes from the Church, or arises from the mandate given to the institute by the Church, there is another type of power in religious communities that arises from the fact that several or many persons live or work together as a community. Its origin is not in the Church, but in the fact of an existing community; that is, its origin is not divine.

In a religious community the main object of government is always to fulfill the mandate given by the Church with a religious aim in sight. In the ordinary, daily life of the community, superiors should, as far as possible, respect the human freedom of the members and let their personalities develop. In this way, a fine balance will be built up in the community. Authority will be mainly concerned with the great religious aim of the institute, with carrying out the mandate of the Church, and with the organization of daily life only so far as that is indispensable for the sake of order and peace. Personal initiative and responsible action in the field of specifically religious work should in no way be excluded, but great weight should be given to legitimate authority. Likewise, real authority in the ordinary running of the community should not be excluded, but the prior aim of the superior should be to leave the member free to develop. In this way, a balance between the realization of the common religious purpose and the development of the freedom of the individual will be established; the two will work together. Moreover, this approach will help to establish a better balance between unity and diversity. While there should be great unity in the main purpose of the institute, corresponding to the mandate received from the Church, there should be great variety in the details of daily life, according to the type of house or community. Such variety will obviously be far less in a monastery than in the house of an apostolic community.

Uniformity, in itself, does not make either the individual or the community more religious. What brings them nearer to God is a way of life in the house which reflects both their common consecration to God and their different personalities.

It is interesting that one of those saints who put much emphasis on obedience, especially as regards the main purpose of the institute, left the greatest discretion to the members in their daily life. St. Ignatius of Loyola did not hesitate to use his power to send men all over the world to propagate the faith; at the same time he left the priests of his Society free to determine the time needed for sleep, the quantity of food, and, possibly with the counsel of the superior or a confessor, the amount of time for prayer that corresponded to their spiritual needs. In all this, Ignatius required discretion, not a uniformity that would have destroyed the spirit of his community. Such an arrangement would not suit the life of a monastery since the monks' chief mission is to continue the prayer of Christ; more uniformity is required to bring beauty and harmony into the celebration of the liturgy.

While it is probably essential theologically, as it is certainly essential legally, to have authority in a religious community in order to achieve full integration into the work of the visible Church, the type of government exercised by authority is not in any way determined by the Church. Authority can be exercised in a corporate way, as in many of the old monastic orders: the community rules on the admission of a novice to profession; the community decides various important issues by majority vote, and the abbot, who is the head of the community, is bound to follow the decision of the majority of the members. It can be exercised in a personal way, as in many orders or congregations founded around the time of the Council of Trent: the superior is infrequently bound to follow the opinion of the community; in fact, frequently he is not legally obliged even to consult it, although Christian charity and prudence may well require him to do so. Between those two systems, there can be many legitimate variations; the Church gives every institute freedom to choose the type of government it wants, either in a more collective or in a more personal way.

When it comes to the exercise of authority at its highest level, that is, at the level of legislation, all religious institutes have a fairly strong collective structure. One does not like to say "democratic" structure because of the word's political connotation, but actually the word democracy as it is understood in civil constitutions would be the nearest equivalent to this system. The general chapters decide the more important questions and make laws by a majority vote. The general superior is usually equivalent to an executive officer who is not entitled to make laws and is subject to the general chapter in all respects. In many modern institutes, personal rule prevails at lower, provincial and local, levels. Personal rule can be enriched by a close cooperation between the head of the community and all the members. In fact, we recognize today that God distributes the graces that he wants to give the community to all the members; therefore, it is necessary that the superior should be in close contact with every member. The wisdom of one man is always less than the wisdom of all the brethren jointly manifest in a Christian and judicious way. To govern any religious institute by the wisdom of only one person would result in great damage; to enlist the wisdom of members may require great skill, but it is indispensible for good government.

RELIGIOUS OBEDIENCE IS MEANINGFUL ONLY IN THE CHURCH

The charisms of virginity or poverty can exist, as we have seen, outside of a religious community. The charism of obedience is essentially a gift that invites a person to incorporate himself more closely into the structure and the life of the visible Church. Obedience is one aspect of consecrated life in community, one of many relations that arise when a person is integrated into a smaller unit of Christ's mystical body. All spiritual graces a Christian receives have an internal dynamism which brings the person into closer contact with the visible Church. The reason for it is in the identity of the Church (spiritual *and* visible) with Christ. The Holy Spirit will gently bring every person nearer to the mystical Christ here on earth.

Virginity is a grace of great internal dynamism, and poverty can be described as flowing from it. The charism of obedience, however, is a distinct step, even if it follows somewhat naturally in many cases. The consecrated person, desiring a more intimate union with Christ, finds it in a closer relationship with the visible Church. Therefore, he asks for admission into a community whose members are all consecrated to God, and which is fully dedicated to works of charity. In all who are called to virginity and poverty, a desire arises to repeat the words and the gestures of Christ, to preach the good news, and to heal the broken hearted, and, in most who are so called, there will also spring up a desire to imitate him within an approved religious community.

Entrance into a community is a complex act: a free person gives himself, and a free community receives him. Rights and duties in the deepest sense come into play on both sides.

This act of entrance takes place when a candidate to religious life pronounces his vows. He promises to serve God in the mystical Christ—that is, the Church. In practice, this act takes place in a community that has been constituted with full approval of the Church and operates under its control. The vow may be pronounced as a vow of obedience to a particular superior, but it is made primarily to the Church. The superior has a right to receive the vow insofar as he represents the Church.

An exchange of promises implicitly takes place when the vow of obedience is made. The religious institute and the superior appear as God's trustees, and they promise, without words (it would be good if they did so expressly), that they will take good material and spiritual care of the candidate. They promise implicitly that they will regard him as a child of God of whom they are trustees, for whom they are responsible to God.

The candidate, in exchange, promises to accept the authority of the Church through the person of the superior. He promises to dedicate himself to the work of the Church through that particular institute, according to its constitutions. This dedication is expressed by the simple words of the vow or promise of obedience. It is a dedication to live and work in an ecclesial community devoted to charity toward each other and toward the whole people of God.

The vow of obedience is, therefore, specifically connected with the visible Church; outside the Church, or independent of it, the vow would have no meaning. This is confirmed by the history of the Church; those Christians who found themselves unable to accept the jurisdiction of the Church rarely favored dedication in obedience, although they may have been completely devoted to poverty, and even to chastity.

If obedience is essentially an ecclesial virtue, a further question arises: what is the immediate object of obedience? This question has two aspects: what is the immediate object of the commands of the superior?; what is the immediate duty of the subject that arises from his commitment?

THE IMMEDIATE OBJECT OF RELIGIOUS OBEDIENCE: TO PARTICIPATE IN CHRIST'S REDEMPTIVE ACTS THROUGH THE CHURCH

The meaning of the existence of the Church is to continue the life of Christ on earth. Christ came to redeem man: this is a specific spiritual purpose. He did not come to judge, but to save; he did not come to abrogate legitimate gifts of personality or of genuine freedom, but to protect them. He came to give and not to take. The meaning of every community in the Church is obviously the same. They exist in order to share this fundamental purpose of the life of the Church, and for no other reason. It follows that anyone who joins a community enters deeply into the saving activity of Christ through the Church. The community has the duty to help the member to share the work of Christ, and the member must be dedicated without reserve to this purpose.

As a consequence, religious government and obedience has, for its primary object, those specifically religious acts that are part of the life of the Church. It follows, also, that other acts of a person who dedicates himself to this community life are secondary objects of government and obedience. Legitimate authority should concern itself with the secondary objects insofar as these are connected with the primary religious activity. If they are not connected, the person should be left free to elect his own course of action. He will not, therefore, be exempt from obedience, but obedience will require him to exercise his freedom.

In this way, a balance is established between the dedication to the work of the Church in a community that requires the offering of the whole man, and the freedom to which he is entitled. Some acts will have no immediate relation to the basic purpose; whether they are done in one way or another is indifferent from the point of view of the primarily dedicated work. Here the question arises as to the right of the individual religious to privacy and to free choice. There would be no virtue and no blessing of obedience if the superior restricted the territory wherein this freedom exists. The superior's commission extends to both: to command when it is necessary and to respect freedom when it is possible. God blesses the exercise of freedom on behalf of the kingdom, for such freedom is always rooted in obedience to God and to the Church.

The practical consequences can be far reaching. It is necessary that one part of the religious' life—that aspect, namely, that refers to ecclesial activity, whether directly or by way of close connection, should be regulated by authority; the other aspect, however—namely that which concerns his private preparation for it—should be respected by the same authority. Simple illustrations could be found in daily activities: the hour of retiring and rising should be prescribed only insofar as it is necessary for a common effort in religious work, and in general, uniformity in the order of the day should be required only insofar as it helps the apostolic work of the community. God blesses diversity just as much as uniformity. (Attention should once more be drawn to the fact that formal obedience to explicit rules and commands will be always more extensive in monastic than in apostolic communities.) This is not to say that a good part of the life of the members of the community is in fact emancipated from the authority of the superior. The religious are under that authority; but the terms of the covenant are that the superior guides their ecclesial activity, and the members, with a certain freedom, adapt the details of their daily life to it. In this sense there is a general duty of obedience on the part of the members, but not an overwhelming and continuous interference with the details of the life of every member of the community by the superior. This is more a balance of charity than of legal rights and duties. The superior has the right to command and the religious the duty to obey because the superior shares the power of the Church and the religious has dedicated himself to the works of the Church. The source of this relationship, and hence of charity, lies in the dedication of the members of a community to the works of Christ in the Church.

Moreover, the right to command and the duty to obey are based on the natural need for order in any community. The source of this relationship is not specifically religious, but it is no less real. It would be wrong, however, to claim that if there is more uniformity in the community, there is necessarily more efficient dedication. Good balance, with few prescriptions, is the ideal, and good balance means a great deal of diversity with substantial unity in the life of the community.

THE GIFT OF APOSTOLIC MISSION

As a rule, religious consecration is expressed by the three vows of chastity, poverty, and obedience, but these three vows can never fully describe the totality of consecrated life. That life is like the light of the sun, which is clear and undivided, and shows no color until it is broken up into its components by a prism. Religious consecration, too, is a unique, undivided gift of God, but it can be broken up into different aspects under theological analysis. The reality of consecration is one and undivided; analysis breaks it up only notionally into different aspects. This oneness or wholeness of the consecration is also revealed by its perpetuity: it cannot be broken up in time, either. Virginity must be perpetual in order to be meaningful; dedication to the following of Christ in poverty must be a commitment for good; dedication to the continuation of the saving work of Christ in the Church and in a community must also be for the whole span of a human life. Otherwise, the covenant with God would not realize its full meaning.

One could think of other vows as possible aids to understanding and expressing more clearly the unique consecration of religious life. In every such consecration, however, another gift is always present: that of an apostolic mission. This mission arises from the fact that the person joins a community that has received a mandate from the Church. The gift of apostolic mission is sometimes expressed, sometimes not. The members of some medieval orders, for example, made a special vow to give themselves for the ransom of captives. In more modern times some orders express this apostolic aspect of their consecration through what is called a fourth vow, which may bind them explicitly to preaching the Gospel to the unbeliever, to teaching children, or nursing the sick. But even if there is no such vow inserted into the constitutions of a religious institute, the apostolic mandate is, nevertheless, operative; all religious communities receive an apostolic mission. They have a commission from the Church; they are sent to carry the Gospel to all men. This statement is valid even for those who consecrate themselves to the exercises of the contemplative life; the very existence of their monastery or community is a dynamic proof to the world of the transcendence of God. Furthermore, the prayer of religious communities, in order to be Christian prayer, must be apostolic. The gift of apostolic charity is present in every consecration; if it were not, there would be no religious consecration. Yet it might be well, sometimes, to make this aspect of consecration explicit, and to add a fourth vow to the other three, in order to bind members to the specific apostolic work of the institute.

It will be long probably before we forget the old classification of religious institutes into contemplative, active, and mixed. The contemplative way of life was frequently presented in the past as the most perfect, since it was expected to lead to deeper union with Christ. The active way of life was identified with apostolic activity, not notably concerned with prayer or recollection. The mixed way of life, too, was claimed to be the most perfect: it was described as based on contemplation but giving an opportunity to pass on to others the fruit of contemplation.

Whatever the merits this classification may have had, it was not accepted by Vatican II, whose vision transcends these categories, and gives a better expression to the reality of consecrated life. That vision can be stated clearly and concisely: all religious are called to contemplation and all have an apostolic mission. The difference between various institutes lies in the modalities of carrying out the basic vocation of contemplation and apostolic action, and not in separating them into contemplative, active, and mixed communities.

All communities are called to contemplation. Here we should not let ourselves be misled by subtle theological distinctions that interpret contemplation in so many different ways. The ideas and the language of Vatican II have, more than once, reflected the simplicity and the terseness of the Gospel. The contemplation referred to by the Fathers is best described by the words of St. Luke about Stephen the Deacon: "Stephen was filled with grace and power" (Acts 6,8), and "Stephen, filled with the Holy Spirit" (Acts 7,55). That is, contemplation means to be filled with the Holy Spirit, with his grace and power, to think, act, and live under the impact of another Person who is the Spirit of God. To this contemplation all religious, without exception, are called, but contemplation should permeate the life of the communities in many different ways. Their way of life should be open to receive the Spirit, their constitutions should favor the materialization of genuine inspirations.

Then the Spirit of God will lead institutes in the same direction, but by many different ways. The fruit of contemplation in every institute will be apostolic action—but not in the same way. Some communities will be led to continue more intensely the solitude of Christ in the desert. Their apostolic activity will consist in erecting monasteries: silent milestones in the history of mankind. The monasteries preach by their very existence and their permanence—they are living symbols of the changeless, silent strength of God; they are witnesses of absolute and eternal values in a continuously changing world. This is not all. The monks have an apostolic action inside the monastery, too, an action that often has an impact on the whole Church. Much of the beauty of the liturgy was born in monasteries; now the whole Church benefits from the devotion of the monks. Moreover, the deep spiritual life of monks has given and gives birth to perpetually valid theological insights that are the treasured possession of the whole Church.

Some other communities will be led to carry on the public ministry of Christ. Their way of life should reflect the simplicity and freshness of the Gospel. Unencumbered by many laws and observances, their heart should be open to the Holy Spirit. In fact, they should be careful not to consume their energy and strength by unnecessary complications under the pretext of "common observance." Not having the protective cloister of the monasteries, they need a free and receptive heart to perceive the inspirations of the Holy Spirit. Ignoring completely the idea that one way of life is "better" or "superior," they can rejoice in following the type of life that our Lord Christ Jesus led, and in which he instructed his apostles. Communities of this type of apostolic life must deeply stress in their spirituality the divine quality of the world—the world as God's house, built for his children. Their liturgy will be the substantial liturgy of creation and redemption, without many external formalities—as was the liturgy of the apostles. As consecrated persons they will move in this world among their fellow men with no less devotion and dedication than a priest would move in the sanctuary, or a monk would celebrate the beauty of the divine office. The gift of apostolic charity, for them, will mean the mission to carry the

living word of God to all creatures, to extend their hands
to the sick, to bless the little ones—continuing the blessing
of Christ. But such communities should not conceive of
their apostolic activity as separate from contemplation: as
the tree has its roots in the ground, so their activity should
have its roots in the Holy Spirit, in his grace and power.
Their life should have the goodness, transparency, and joy
of the life of the twelve apostles. Legalism can be a great
enemy of such a simple life; they should remember how
many times Christ warned his apostles against it. Too
many laws can cloud the vision of the heart, just as a complete lack of law can leave a person in the dark.

Let us say again that the gift of apostolic mission belongs to all communities. It is the charism of every consecrated person, no less than chastity, poverty, or obedience. There is no hierarchy among the various "ways of
life"; no one is superior to the other. All religious are
called to silent contemplation and creative apostolic action, but within this general call every community has its
own way of life. All these ways are holy, and they reflect
the glory and the wealth of the Spirit in their great variety.
So far as they have their origin in the inspiration of the
Spirit, each is unique and irreplaceable. Each one reflects
the mystery of the incarnation: the silent union of Christ
with his Father and his work for our redemption.

NEW LITURGY OF RELIGIOUS CONSECRATION

Our theological reflections have brought to the surface the
essential elements in religious life. We have seen that it is a
gift of God; it has manifold aspects; it includes the offer of
God's companionship, the gift of the possession of the

earth, the invitation to continue the saving work of Christ in a visible religious community, and the gift of apostolic charity.

All these gifts come from God. In the beginning they are more like a promise, a mustard seed, but later they must become a strong reality, a great tree. It is desirable that the ceremony of admission into a religious order should fully express this divine generosity. If someone says simply, "I am taking the vows of chastity, poverty, and obedience," he is telling only half the truth, or perhaps not even that much. The reality is that he is receiving a gift from God, and he has no power over that gift. All he can do is accept it or, to his own great damage, reject it, but he can not create the gift. Therefore, any ceremony of admission should make clear that the gift is from God.

The giving of a gift from God through the visible Church is beautifully expressed by the ceremony of the imposition of hands in the consecration of a priest. There, of course, a sacrament is given to the candidate; when a religious is consecrated, no sacrament is given. Still, it would be more fitting if, somehow, the whole ceremony emphasize that it is God who is the principal giver, and that man is only accepting the divine gift. Externally, this act of giving could be expressed by the imposition of hands, or by the imposition of a veil, and by the candidate's declaring that he accepts the divine gifts and, therefore, promises virginity, poverty, obedience, and apostolic charity. There is a covenant between God and man; God has taken the initiative. The ceremony or the liturgy is perfect only when it reflects this reality with clarity and simplicity.

This consecration takes place in a religious community. It would therefore be well if there could be an expression of another covenant that is entered into also. It is the religious superior who, in the name of the Church, hands over a grace to the person and accepts his dedication in that community. It would be true and realistic if the religious superior would promise, in the name of the Church and of his community, to receive the candidate in Christ's name, to honor him as a member of Christ, and to take care of him as he would take care of Christ himself. In his turn, the candidate should promise a full and loving dedication to the work of Christ in this institute according to its constitutions. There is nothing exaggerated in this: if a community honors Christ in a guest, how much more they should find him in a new member. And the new member should find Christ in the visible Church, of which the community is a living organ.

Thus, apart from the divine covenant, which is primary, there would be this secondary covenant and exchange of promises between the human superior in the Church and the person seeking admission into the community. The divine covenant is unilateral—it is God who gives, man who receives. The human covenant is bilateral —both parties give and both will be bound, one might say, until death do them part.

Such a ceremony would correspond to some of the ancient traditions of the Church, as the traditional way of consecrating virgins. It would correspond also to a spiritual and temporal reality in which the community and the person mutually promise fidelity.

THE CHARISM OF A RELIGIOUS INSTITUTE

All charisms are primarily personal; they are the gifts of God to a person. When he gives the same charism to many persons and they come together, a community is established, led by the same purpose and nourished from the same source. In this sense, we can speak about the charism of a community, of a religious institute. The Holy Spirit is leading all members in the same direction.

It would be difficult to describe all the types of charism that can be given to different religious communities, but there is one fundamental distinction among charisms that must be emphasized: there are charisms given in view of the universal Church, and charisms given in view of local churches.

Sometimes it pleased God to give to a community a gift from which the whole Church benefited. The charisms of St. Benedict, St. Francis of Assisi, and St. Ignatius expanded over the earth, and brought blessings to the whole world; their gift had a relation to the universal Church. Since such gifts come from the Holy Spirit, the Church itself is duty-bound to accept and honor them, once the gift has been duly examined and proved to be authentic. Such a community with gifts for the universal Church should be subject to universal jurisdiction of the Holy See.

A charism can be given also to an institute mainly destined to bring forth fruit in a given region, or in a given land. A religious community may receive the vocation to preach the Gospel in Africa, and in Africa only. Again, such a vocation has to be respected by the Church, after it is proved to come from the Holy Spirit. It is right and just that a community with such a gift should be subject to the jurisdiction of an organ which has power over the whole region where the religious work. Otherwise, the work of the whole institute would be hampered, and their charism would not achieve its full effect.

It is possible also for a community to receive a gift to

be at the service of a local Church, of a diocese. Such a community should be subject to the local authority, the bishop of the diocese. It is in this way that their charism and their gift will produce the best fruit; to go any further might destroy the specific gift.

It would be wrong for those who have a vocation to help the universal Church to tie themselves down with local worries; they would lose their flexibility and mobility. It would be equally wrong for those who receive the gift of stability in one place to try to expand into other places which were not intended for them.

These suggestions consider the religious in relation to the episcopal body. Some of the religious institutes with a universal mission would be subject to the universal body, represented by its head, the Pope. Some of them with a regional or national mission would be subject to the regional or national episcopal conference. Some of them, having a specific mission within a diocese, would be subject to a residential bishop. The somewhat ugly word of exemption could disappear; instead of exemption, there would be subjection to the episcopal college or to its various organs or members. In this way, religious would be incorporated into the structure of the Church.

RELIGIOUS VOCATION AND THE VOCATION OF A DIOCESAN PRIEST

At this point in our explanation, it can be enlightening to consider what is common and what is different in the vocation of a religious and of a diocesan priest. Obviously there are common elements. Religious are consecrated in virginity and in poverty. Diocesan priests, in the present discipline of the Latin Church, are consecrated to the priesthood only if they promise or accept celibacy. The Council also made it clear that each diocesan priest has the vocation to Christian poverty, to the use of created things in a dedicated way. It follows that virginity and poverty are common elements in both vocations, although the source of obligation is not fully identical in both cases: religious take explicit and public vows, diocesan priests dedicate themselves implicitly to an evangelical way of life.

The main difference between the vocation of a religious and a diocesan priest is seen in the manner of their incorporation into the visible Church. A religious community exists because it has received a mission from the Church, and a person who has a religious vocation is integrated, incorporated in a special way into the visible Church through this community by sharing its religious mission. The work of a religious is related to the visible Church through his community. He receives the grace of his consecration from the Church through the community.

This is not so with the diocesan priest. His incorporation into the visible Church is in his immediate relationship with a diocesan bishop. He does not join a community in order to be subject, through it, to the episcopal body or to an organ of it or to a member of it; rather, he enters into immediate relationship with the bishop. His dedication to the visible Church will be in assisting the bishop, not in being a member of a community.

From this difference it follows that while a religious will be governed by the superior of his community and will show obedience to that superior, a diocesan priest will be governed by the bishop and will show obedience to the bishop. There might be some difference in degree in this government and obedience, but there is no difference in kind; in both cases we are dealing with a consecrated type of relationship. The relationship established between a religious and his superior is consecrated by a vow; the one established between a bishop and his priest springs from sacerdotal consecration. In both cases there is a sacred relationship from which obedience originates, but, in one instance, it is obedience in a community, in the other, immediately to an individual.

It may be useful to recall that in both cases the principal meaning and the primary purpose of the relationship between the superior and the subject is the continuation of the saving work of Christ. But the sphere of government extends in a more general way over the whole person of the religious, because he is dedicated in a community to the work of the visible Church, while the sphere of government is not so broadly extended for the diocesan priest. Since he does not live in a community, his work is more personal. In both cases, however, the proper and immediate object of government and obedience is the work of the Church. Any other activity of the religious, and even of the diocesan priest, falls under the power of the superior because of its relation to this specifically religious work of the Church.

Briefly, the greatest difference between the two vocations, religious life and diocesan priesthood, lies in the type of incorporation of the person into the structure of the visible Church. For a religious, it is through community; for a diocesan priest, it is through a person-to-person relationship with his bishop. This explanation seems to mean that there is not much difference between the two vocations. In reality there is not a great deal of difference between them—at least it is not as great as has sometimes been suggested in the past; but this proves, perhaps, the correctness of the explanation. Both vocations, religious and diocesan, harmoniously fit with the theory and the theory corresponds to the facts. Both groups, religious and diocesan priests, are called to holiness; both have a function in the visible Church, but in a different way.

PERSONAL SANCTITY

A question about religious life is frequently asked: Is the grace of religious vocation given for the sanctification of the person who receives it, or is it given for the sanctification of the Church? If it is for the sanctification of the person only, the primary aim of a consecrated person, or of a community of consecrated persons, is not apostolic. They are to seek first their own sanctification, and it is only secondarily that they can give their time to the people of God. If, however, the primary aim of religious life is to fulfill a mission in the Church, the gifts included in the consecration are not principally for the sanctification of the person, but have to be used as signs that lead the people of God to their Lord.

The question, put in the form of this dilemma, is misleading. It supposes a perfect division between the two types of grace: those given for the sanctification of the individual and those given for the good of the whole body. It does not take into account the organic nature of the Church and the fact that every member is incorporated, integrated into the whole body.

Looking back at our salvation history, we find that any grace given by God to his chosen ones had a double aspect and a double effect which can hardly be divided, even notionally. Abraham was chosen to be a friend of

God and the father of all believers. He had a mission to fulfill, that of receiving God's covenant for a new people. At the same time he was a friend of God.

It was the same with King David. God gave him an historic mission, to reunite the dispersed tribes of Israel into one nation. At the same time, God showered his personal favors on him and, in spite of David's failures, God made him holy. Also, when the fulness of time came, Mary of Nazareth was chosen to be the Mother of God—a mission above every other mission given to a creature by God—and she was sanctified more and in a deeper way than any other human person. The grace of the apostles also had this double aspect; they were chosen in view of a mission, and Jesus called them his own beloved friends.

In God's plan, the two aspects and effects of grace, the personal and the corporate, cannot be separated. To be a friend of God means to have a mission in the world, and to have a mission in the world means to be a friend of God. The two aspects are one, like soul and body; or even more, because they cannot be separated. If a separation took place, grace would be destroyed. This deep unity is there because every friend of God is incorporated into the Church, and any grace and gift given to him redounds immediately to the good of the Church, internally and externally. Every mission given by God to a person for the sanctification of the Church sanctifies the very same person first: if he has to distribute strength, he must have strength himself.

The consequences for religious persons and communities are of some import. Every religious is a friend of God, but precisely because he is a friend of God, he has a mission in the world to make God's name known to all men. This mission means a grace, and grace touches his heart first. Even before sanctifying the Church, grace sanctifies him—this religious person. It is the same with every religious community. A community receives its common charism for both its own sanctification and the building of the Church. The holier the community is, the more it is able to witness the living presence of Christ among men and be a sign that leads to eternal life.

THE FUTURE OF RELIGIOUS LIFE

Are religious still needed in the Church, or should we admit that the age of their usefulness is over and that God wants to distribute his graces in a different way?

It will be easier to answer this question now, at the conclusion of our reflections, than it would have been in the beginning. Religious life is the existential gift of God to his Church; it is the fruit of God's dynamic action in the Church. Therefore, any question about the future of religious life is a question about the future of God's active abundance in the Church, about the dynamic action of the Holy Spirit among his people. In reality, the right way to put the question should be: is it likely that God will continue to distribute the charisms of his special companionship, of the possession of the earth, and of the dedication to the work of the Church in a community, or will he cease to distribute these charisms?

It is evident that the problem concerns God's mysterious action, and we do not have a revelation of God's own plans. We can describe God's action in the past, and say that from the beginning of the Church, he has given his companionship in a special way to men and women who remained virgins. The first among them was Mary of Nazareth; the last one is probably just about to ask for admission into a novitiate. Between these two there is an infinite number of consecrated men and women. From the beginning, God has given to many freedom from the captivity of earthly possessions. Again, Mary of Nazareth was the first to receive this gift, and the apostles followed; the last one is perhaps a hidden person who is going to work among the poorest people in a large city. Also, from an early time, communities of charismatic persons arose—first in the East, then in the West—communities that had an organic structure. The members were helped and directed by a person who presided over the group. One after another, structured institutes emerged in East and West. Christian tradition brought out the value of dedication in these ecclesial communities and praised the virtue of obedience. There is no doubt about God's action in the past; we can even see the fruit of it in the present. But what about the future?

It would be tempting to say that we have to admit our ignorance about the future. After all, who can foresee what God is going to do? Religious life is not part of the essential structure of the Church; therefore, it could disappear.

Yet, it would be poor theology to evade an answer on the ground of ignorance. We are not in ignorance, not fully, at any rate. If religious life is God's existential gift to the Church, it is not subject to human power. If God wants to give it, the Church has a duty to accept it—a fact affirmed by the Council in the Constitution on the Church. If God gave this gift in the past, he is not likely to deprive his Church of it in the future. God revealed himself, his free creative action, something of his artistic and poetic beauty, through the inspirations from which the great variety of religious communities arose: one proclaiming the prayer of Christ, another declaring Christ's poverty, another again carrying Christ's words to the ends of the earth. It is a legitimate assumption, even for our limited intellect and vision, that what God did in the past, he is likely to do in the future.

It is said that the beginning of theology is wonder and admiration: wonder in the presence of a divine mystery, and admiration of God's mighty deeds. The theology of religious life is precisely this—wonder in seeing the fruits of the presence of the Holy Spirit among his people, and admiration in perceiving his strength in men and women. It is good theology to say that as God has acted in the past, he is likely to act in the future; therefore, the future of religious life is the future of God's dynamic, creative action in the Church, and there is a great future for that.

There is perhaps an even deeper reason for saying that religious life will exist in the Church for a long time to come, even until the end of time. The Church is the living Christ. Its being, its work, expresses the various aspects of Christ's life. In the Church the mystery of the incarnation is present. The Church reflects the hidden divinity of Christ and carries the limitations of human nature. It is to be expected that as God marked the birth of his son according to the flesh by the gift of virginity, by the gift of poverty, and by the gift of obedience and living charity, so he will mark his Church by the same gifts.

As virginity belonged to the pattern of the incarnation, in the earthly life of Christ, it will belong to the pattern of the life of Christ in the Church. The gift of virginity will be distributed by God to those whom he chooses to love in this particular way. As the life of Christ was marked by the possession of the earth (which was expressed sometimes in deep poverty), the life of the Church, too, will have to be marked by poverty of heart and sometimes by external poverty. As Christ in his mortal life became obedient and subjected himself for his Father's sake to human persons and to created agents, so there has to be obedience in the Church. Those who continue the saving work of Christ in a religious community, become obedient and subject themselves to human persons for the sake of the kingdom of God.

The pattern of the incarnation of Christ is reproduced in a striking way in the structure of religious life in the Church. God has kept alive these gifts of virginity, poverty, obedience, and living charity in the Church since the very beginning. Because of the union of Christ with his Church this pattern will accompany and mark the Church until the end of time. There will always be virgins; there will always be men poor in heart following Christ; there will always be communities dedicated to the work of the Church and accepting a covenant from the living Christ, the Head of the Church. To say that religious life is likely to remain in the Church is to declare the permanency of the pattern of the incarnation.

Obviously, such judgments are valid for the substance of religious life and not for its accidental structures. The external structures are subject to change. We saw them emerging in the course of history; we saw some of them disappear. The divine element is permanent; the human element is subject to development. The wisdom of religious today consists in keeping what is divine in their gifts and inserting it into the new human framework that is needed for our age. Religious received light and love from God; now it is time to make these gifts known to all. Christ's words are for them:

> You are the light of the world. A city built on a hill-top cannot be hidden. No one lights a lamp to put it under a tub; they put it on the lamp-stand where it shines for everyone in the house. In the same way your light must shine in the sight of men, so that seeing your good works, they may give the praise to your Father in heaven (Mt 5, 14–16).

2

God's Companionship: Virginity

Whenever the documents of Vatican II refer to con-secrated life and mention the three evangelical counsels, chastity takes priority over poverty and obedience. In establishing this new, or apparently new, order, the fathers of the Council followed an ancient tradition and also set in clearer focus the internal cohesion between the three counsels. They returned to the ancient tradition because, from the beginning of the life of the Church, consecrated virginity was considered the sign and fruit of a special friendship with God. They more clearly focused the internal cohesion of the three aspects of religious consecration, because virginity establishes a special union between God and a human person. Detachment from material wealth in the form of poverty usually follows the charism of virginity. Both charisms can produce greater fruit if they are inserted into the life of the visible community, which is, in effect, consecration in obedience. Among the three, chastity is nearest to charity; it is the most personal expression of our dedication to God.

Before any further development of these ideas, it is necessary to clarify terminology. Two key concepts must be defined: chastity and virginity.

Chastity is a virtue that disposes one to the observance of God's laws in all matters concerning sexual life. It is necessary for both the unmarried and the married. When a person abstains from marriage it is frequently said that he is practicing *perfect* chastity, meaning that he abstains completely from any use of his sexual faculties. The expression is proper, provided that one does not conclude that the virtue of chastity cannot be perfect in married people; they can practice it perfectly although their abstinence from sexual life is not complete.

The term virginity usually means perfect chastity in those who preserve the integrity of their body. One could object to this definition on the ground that virginity is thus conceived of in too material a sense. It would be better to emphasize the spiritual sense of virginity, which means dedication to God in perfect chastity with the intention of preserving integrity of mind and body. Christian virginity, in the full sense, means a permanent state, the permanent integrity of mind, heart, and body for the sake of the kingdom of God. It is a spiritual virtue. It disposes for a deep union with God, and it is the fruit of such a union. Its most important aspect is not the material integrity of the body—that of itself is not necessarily a sign of Christian virginity—but the integrity and the permanent dedication of the person to God in perfect chastity.

In other words, there is not much difference between perfect chastity and virginity, provided "integrity" means the integral dedication of a person in mind, heart, and body to God. To remain faithful to the tradition of Christian terminology, it would probably be better to speak about virginity than about chastity; therefore, the term virginity will be used for perfect chastity in what follows.

Virginity refers equally to men and women, and when the term celibate is used, it is equivalent to virgin.

THE BIBLICAL BACKGROUND

The inspiration from Holy Scripture for an understanding of the virtue of virginity flows in two channels: the express pronouncements of the inspired texts about virginity, and the example of Christ, his Mother, and his disciples. The biblical doctrine of an experiential union with God undoubtedly helps toward a better understanding of virginity. This union can so captivate a human heart that the person does not desire to contract any close union with a fellow human being. The presence of God in him brings about a special fruit: he wants to remain virgin.

Some express pronouncements in the Old Testament about virginity are found in the life of Jeremiah who remained celibate in order to authenticate his prophecy. In the New Testament the main texts about virginity are in the Gospels of St. Matthew and St. Luke, in the epistles of St. Paul, and in the Apocalypse of St. John. All through the Scriptures there is an ever deepening emphasis on this virtue. The life of Christ, the life of the Mother of God, and the lives of many of the apostles are in themselves demonstrations of the Christian virtue of virginity.

The express references to virginity in the Bible will be supplemented by some allusions to the union from which virginity originates.

Jeremiah the Prophet. The concept of virginity developed gradually. Its earliest roots are in the Old Testament; Christian virginity is somewhat foreshadowed in the life of Jeremiah. The prophet embraced celibacy and explained the reason for it:

> The word of Yahweh was addressed to me as follows: "You must not take a wife or have son or daughter in this place. For Yahweh says this regarding the sons and daughters to be born in this place, about the mothers who give birth to them, and about the fathers who beget them in this land: They will die of deadly diseases . . ." (Jer 16, 1–4).

Jeremiah's celibacy was a prophecy by deed: he was announcing to the people of Jerusalem that the day of judgment was coming. In order to underline the proximity of the disaster, Jeremiah did not take a wife. Through his celibacy he was crying out that the judgment of the Lord was coming and that all should be prepared for it.

Paul the Prophet. The same theme is taken up in the New Testament by St. Paul. He is not concerned with the destruction of Jerusalem, but rather with the second coming of the Lord, with the universal manifestation of his glory. Paul is so full of hope that he wants to bypass the realities of this present world of shadows in order to center his attention on the expectation of the Lord. He writes to the Corinthians:

> About remaining celibate, I have no directions from the Lord but give my own opinion as one who, by the Lord's mercy, has stayed faithful. Well then, I believe that in these present times of stress this is right: that it is good for a man to stay as he is (1 Cor 7, 25–26).

The "present times of stress" arose from the fact that the early Christians were expecting the Parousia, the day of judgment, the day of the manifestation of the power of the Lord. The underlying idea in Paul's statement is that the very fact that he remains a celibate declares, not in words but in deed, that the really permanent values are in a different world. The prophetic aspect of celibacy is present in Paul's thought, but while Jeremiah was concerned in a somewhat negative way with the temporal ruin of Jerusalem, Paul is centered on the coming of the eternal kingdom of Christ. Through celibacy he declares that his world is to be transformed into a new spiritual universe.

Matthew and the Kingdom. In the Gospel of St. Matthew the internal relationship between the state of virginity and the kingdom of God is described. The most important passage on celibacy follows the promulgation by Christ of the new law: a man should not divorce his wife. Then:

> The disciples said to him, "If that is how things are between husband and wife, it is not advisable to marry." But he replied, "It is not everyone who can accept what I have said, but only those to whom it is granted. There are eunuchs born that way from their mother's womb, there are eunuchs made so by men and there are eunuchs who have made themselves that way for the sake of the kingdom of heaven. Let anyone accept this who can" (Mt 19, 10–12).

The key concept of the text is that abstinence from marriage receives its full meaning when it is practiced on behalf of the heavenly kingdom. There is a close relationship between the kingdom of Christ and the state of celibacy or virginity, and Paul declares that no one can embrace this state on his own initiative. It is given to those who are able to accept what God offers them; in other words, celibacy is a gift of God.

Matthew means by the kingdom of heaven the fulfillment of God's promises, the presence of the kingdom
foretold by the prophets, announced by John the Baptist,
preached by Christ, and to be preached by the apostles.
Celibacy in itself would be empty and without purpose; it
receives its meaning through the kingdom, which means
both the internal kingdom in the hearts of man and the
kingdom to be spread through the preaching of the Gospel. When a gift is given on behalf of the kingdom, all
aspects of the kingdom must be included. The gift is given
to dispose the heart to receive the Word of God, and to
strengthen the person to preach it. Both the sanctifying
and the strongly apostolic aspects of virginity are set forth
in Christ's words as reported by Matthew.

This kingdom is partially present because Christ is
present and he opened his kingdom to all who repent and
are ready to follow him. It is likewise a kingdom to come
because the Spirit had not yet descended on the apostles
and disciples. The concept of virginity in Matthew's
Gospel is complex: virginity witnesses to a present reality,
and points to a future event. It is the sign of the kingdom
present, and of the kingdom to come. The kingdom is
present; for its sake one can be celibate; there is no need to
wait. At the same time the prophetic value remains, since
the fullness of God's promises is still to come. Celibacy
points towards eschatological fullness or perfection; one
could say that, in the life of a celibate person, reality and
prophecy coincide.

Virginity is a sign of the kingdom present here and
now and of the kingdom to come when Christ appears in
his glory. Let us note that virginity is not a condition for
entering the kingdom; it is rather a special gift *within* the

kingdom for those who can accept it. Matthew makes it
clear that he conceives of celibacy as a particular gift given
by God to some who are following Christ and are his disciples. Not all followers and all disciples will be granted that
gift.

In another passage, Matthew reports the saying of
Christ that in the resurrection there is no marrying or
being given in marriage: "For at the resurrection men and
women do not marry; no, they are like angels in heaven"
(Mt 22, 30). In other words, the state of virginity is the
beginning of the same state of life in some which will be
the share of all who will enter the heavenly kingdom. In
heaven there will be no need for procreation because the
number of the chosen ones will have been completed. The
kingdom of God will be there in its fullness. Marriage
would be purposeless. It follows that the state of virginity
is the beginning of the state of immortality. Through it a
person enters even in this world into what is destined to
be his final status in the kingdom of God.

Luke and the Following of Christ. Luke leads us
even further into the mystery of virginity. For him, as for
Matthew, the kingdom of God has come with Christ, but
Luke gives more thought to the relationship of a disciple
to Christ; to the union that exists between Christ and his
follower. Luke considers virginity as the sharing in a special way of the death and the glorification of Christ. "Special way" here means that virginity is a particular vocation,
one not given to all believers. The most important text is:

> He said to them, "I tell you solemnly, there is no one
> who has left house, wife, brothers, parents or children for
> the sake of the kingdom of God who will not be given

repayment many times over in this present time and, in
the world to come, eternal life" (Lk 18, 29–30).

He who follows Christ by leaving his wife, that is, by
embracing the state of celibacy, leaves this world and enters another. He shares the condition of Christ who leaves
this world to enter into the house of his Father. The person who leaves his wife and all that he has in this world,
shares the death of Christ. Another text from St. Luke
proves that this is not an exaggeration:

> If any man comes to me without hating his father, mother,
> wife, children, brothers, sisters, yes and his own life too,
> he cannot be my disciple. Anyone who does not carry his
> cross and come after me cannot be my disciple (Lk 14,
> 26–27).

There is an analogy, therefore, between leaving one's
wife and family and taking up the cross, an analogy between celibacy and leaving one's own life and dying with
Christ. To follow Christ means to leave this visible and
tangible world, and the persons or objects most precious
to us, and to go into an unknown world. In Luke's Gospel
the theology of the life of a Christian as life in Christ is
emerging. It is necessary to be united to Christ's cross in
order to participate in his eternal life. Finally, as in Matthew's Gospel, so in Luke's, the kingdom has a dynamic
character: it has to grow and expand. To become celibate
for the kingdom's sake means to share in the building of
the kingdom, in the saving acts of Christ—celibacy has an
apostolic character and finality.

Paul and the Glory of God.   The new theme of sharing the glory of Christ through virginity is best expressed
by St. Paul; although he proclaims that marriage is good
and, indeed, holy, he continues:

I would like to see you free from all worry. An unmarried man can devote himself to the Lord's affairs, all he need worry about is pleasing the Lord; but a married man has to bother about the world's affairs and devote himself to pleasing his wife: he is torn two ways. In the same way an unmarried woman, like a young girl, can devote herself to the Lord's affairs; all she need worry about is being holy in body and spirit. The married woman, on the other hand, has to worry about the world's affairs and devote herself to pleasing her husband. I say this only to help you, not to put a halter round your necks, but simply to make sure that everything is as it should be, and that you give your undivided attention to the Lord (1 Cor 7, 32–35).

How to be holy in body and spirit: the word *holy* is the key to understanding the text. Paul uses the word according to the Old Testament tradition. Anything is holy which has been sanctified by God through the presence of his glory and power. For the Israelites, Mount Sinai was holy because the glory of God descended on it; the temple of Jerusalem was holy because the presence of God overshadowed its inner sanctuary, the Holy of Holies. A person who receives the gift of virginity is holy because the power and glory of God descends on him and consecrates him.

According to Paul's thought, the temple of Jerusalem had no more meaning, for the sacrifices of the Old Covenant had come to an end and the holiness of God left the temple. Now God's holiness resides in every Christian and those who have received the gift of virginity are particularly able to sense it and to respond to it. Their lives belong to the new cult of a new age, the age of the Spirit; they are overshadowed by the divine presence that they now experience. In their lives a new cult, a new liturgy emerges, similar to that which will be the cult and liturgy of the eternal and immortal kingdom of God. In this sense the soul and body of a celibate person has been assumed into the spiritual kingdom of God.

Another approach to the theology of St. Paul on marriage and virginity can be made through the Epistle to the Ephesians. Since for St. Paul marriage belongs to this transient world, and is a temporal institution, it can stand as a symbol or sign of Christ's union with his Church. Paul employs an earthly reality, marriage, to demonstrate and illustrate a heavenly mystery. Virginity is not an earthly reality, therefore it cannot be taken to illustrate something final. Virginity is a final reality in itself; it is the final state of God's chosen ones. It cannot serve as a symbol for anything else.

In the virgin the mystery of the resurrection is already present and dynamic because his soul and body have been consecrated by the Holy Spirit. Paul frequently states that it was the Spirit of the Father who raised Christ from the dead. It is the same Spirit who gives new life to a human person, vivifies him through the gift of virginity, raises him from this world, and gives him the power and glory of the world to come. The life of virgins is analogous to the life of God's blessed ones in heaven.

Virginity and Our Redemption. To the analysis of these many texts a substantial remark should be added: the four Gospels, the epistles, and the other documents of the New Testament literally breathe the atmosphere of virginity. At their center is Christ who was virgin. He was born of a woman who remained virgin, and the Apostle John, whom Jesus especially loved, was a virgin. Finally, Paul, perhaps the most dynamic among the apostles, declared his intention to remain celibate. In St. John's Revelation the elect are described as virgins who are near the throne of the Lamb; the text is an eminent testimony of the esteem the early Church had for virginity:

> Next in my vision I saw Mount Zion, and standing on it a Lamb who had with him a hundred and forty-four thousand people, all with his name and his Father's name written on their foreheads. I heard a sound coming out of the sky like the sound of the ocean or the roar of thunder; it seemed to be the sound of harpists playing their harps. There in front of the throne they were singing a new hymn in the presence of the four animals and the elders, a hymn that could only be learnt by the hundred and forty-four thousand who had been redeemed from the world. These are the ones who have kept their virginity and not been defiled with women; they follow the Lamb wherever he goes; they have been redeemed from amongst men to be the first-fruits for God and for the Lamb. They never allowed a lie to pass their lips and no fault can be found in them (Rev 14, 1–5).

SOME THEOLOGICAL PRINCIPLES

Christian virginity is so closely connected with the incarnation, with the distribution of graces in the Church, and with the presence of eternal life here on earth that it has something of the nature of a mystery. It cannot therefore be fully explained by concepts and definitions, although these can be of help. Images and symbols from our Christian tradition, however, can take over where notional knowledge ends, and they can convey a deeper understanding of God's gift.

Some clear theological principles will help to prepare the ground for this understanding:

(a) Christian virginity is not identical with supernatural charity. If it were, the kingdom of God would be reserved for virgins alone, but the kingdom is open to all men of good will whether they be married or virgins. Since charity is infused into our hearts by the Spirit, every man called to live by charity is called to live in the Spirit. Therefore, union with the Spirit of God is not the privilege of virgins only; all are called to divine union.

(b) Virginity removes some "obstacles which might draw a person away from the fervor of charity and the perfection of divine worship" (*Lumen Gentium* in Abbott, *op. cit.*, p. 74). Although this is a negative principle, it has real significance. It implies that virginity is a dying to this world in order to be raised to another one. Such dying is necessary because the internal dynamism of a human person is far from being fully balanced. In many cases it centers on human persons and on temporal cares with such an intensity that it is not able to rise to a generous love of God. The mystery of the cross shines through this apparently negative principle.

(c) Virginity helps a person derive more fruit from his baptismal grace. It is not itself the baptismal grace; Christians are baptized for a life of charity, and not of virginity; but virginity can help to develop the baptismal grace by creating an internal dynamism which turns a human person fully and continuously toward Christ and eternal life. A human heart can be great enough to love God alone. Virginity adds a certain alertness and sensitivity to the inspirations of the Holy Spirit, a certain readiness to follow them.

(d) Virginity is the fruit of baptismal grace. There is no spiritual gift which is not rooted in some way in the baptismal grace, in the personal presence of the Spirit in a

Christian. Virginity is a special fruit given to some and not to all. The reason why it is given to a determined person is hidden in the depths of God's designs, but since the gift of virginity is rooted in the baptismal grace, it carries the mark of Christ's death and resurrection.

MAN WAS CREATED TO HAVE A COMPANION

To balance these abstract principles it is good to turn to a basic fact of human life: God made man to have a companion. This need is built into a person's body and soul; it comes from God himself, and no man can change it: "The Lord God said, 'It is not good that the man should be alone. I will make him a helpmate' " (Gen 2, 18).

This need is fulfilled in marriage, which is a deep personal union between man and woman. They become one flesh, as St. Paul says, and, what is even more important, they should become one spirit. The physical union of their bodies should be an expression of their spiritual union. Marriage is not perfect unless the union extends to the minds, hearts, and bodies of the two persons; and when this union exists, it becomes so absorbing, so absolute that it excludes any similar union with a different person. Mutual fidelity is a consequent duty of this union.

The union in marriage is holy. Christ himself made it a sacrament, and St. Paul has chosen it to be the symbol of Christ's union with the Church. Marriage is, in fact, so good and so fulfilling for a man and for a woman that it would be unwise to avoid it in ordinary circumstances. It can be wise, however, to accept a call from a divine Person who promises love and companionship in a way that no human being can give.

GOD OFFERS HIMSELF AS A COMPANION TO A HUMAN PERSON

From the fact that man was created to have a companion, we now turn to an existential event. It is the irruption of a new experience into a human life: God offers himself to be the one and exclusive companion of a human person. This happens in a new encounter between God and man; it is the offer of a covenant. Let us examine its terms.

Companionship has a special sense in this context. God is the friend of every Christian, of every human being. Sometimes, however, he wants to establish a special friendship, a refreshing and exhilarating oneness through a personal conversation or dialog, through the communication of his knowledge and of his love, through a union that excludes distractions and the planting of roots too deep in this world. A person will not be immediately holier because of this offer, but he will have a source of holiness if he accepts God's gift in faith and fidelity.

The companionship offered carries the seal of God's immensity; he reveals something of his wealth and riches. He does not mislead the person, for from the beginning of the offer it is clear that he is a spiritual being, and his friendship moves on a transcendent plane. What he offers is a communion in his Spirit, the sharing of divine things in a divine way. The offer attracts the whole human person; it appears as satisfying the deepest of human aspirations. It is an experience of God's presence, it is overwhelming, and it takes possession of a human person. Jeremiah's words in his confessions could be applied to it: "You have seduced me, Yahweh, and I have let myself be seduced; you have overpowered me: you were the stronger." (Jer 20, 7).

When God concludes this special companionship with

a man, any other deep union with a human being, as happens in marriage, is excluded. The result of God's invitation, or, to use the biblical term, of God's seduction, is that a new type of spiritual union is effected between God and man. A personal conversation, a dialog, begins, by which knowledge and love are communicated and man is enriched. But, since a human being is limited, he cannot enter into another union, the human union that is marriage, which in its own way would also be deep and absorbing. Therefore, the right conclusion of this special visitation of God is consecration in virginity.

Virginity becomes the fruit of God's call, the framework of God's presence, and the best disposition to hear God's words in silence. Through virginity, the heart and mind, the soul and body are established in a silence, in a sensitivity, in which communication with God is made easier. No wonder, then, that a man in these circumstances does not desire to enter into marriage.

God's companionship is, of course, spiritual; but the spiritual grace is infused into the whole person, into soul and body as *one*; and it begins to give a new balance to the whole man, including his body. That is why a man who has no companion according to the law of his nature, can be happy, balanced, and relaxed: the spiritual gift holds the whole person in equilibrium.

RETURN TO THE BIBLE: MARY AND PAUL

The specific gift of virginity consists in a particular strength that balances the natural instincts of the body in a spiritual way. A description of this call and of this communication of strength is given by St. Luke through the words of Mary in the *Magnificat,* in which she declares that she experienced the communication of a particular strength from God which kept her virgin and made her mother. Therefore she is full of joy and praises God:

> And Mary said:
> My soul proclaims the greatness of the Lord and my spirit exults in God my savior; because he has looked upon his lowly handmaid. Yes, from this day forward all generations will call me blessed, for the Almighty has done great things for me. Holy is his name, and his mercy reaches from age to age for those who fear him. He has shown the power of his arm, he has routed the proud of heart. He has pulled down princes from their thrones and exulted the lowly. The hungry he has filled with good things, the rich sent empty away. He has come to the help of Israel his servant, mindful of his mercy —according to the promise he made to our ancestors—of his mercy to Abraham and to his descendants for ever (Lk 1, 46–55).

A sense of fulfillment, of elation, of deep gratitude breathes through this prayer which proclaims that the Creator and his creature have found each other in a new relationship. Without this experience of a new type of union with God which is a communication of strength, no one could ever declare that he wished to be a virgin.

Paul also describes the effect of this call and of this communication of strength:

> I would like to see you free from all worry. An unmarried man can devote himself to the Lord's affairs, all he need worry about is pleasing the Lord; but a married man has to bother about the world's affairs and devote himself to pleasing his wife: he is torn two ways. In the same way an unmarried woman, like a young girl, can devote herself to the Lord's affairs; all she need worry about is being holy in body and spirit. The married woman, on the other

hand, has to worry about the world's affairs and devote herself to pleasing her husband (1 Cor 7, 32–34).

What Paul is saying is that unmarried men and women receive a new freedom to enjoy God's presence—his glory and his power in them. They are also free to plan how to bring the message of the Gospel to others. A new strength frees them from human bonds and gives them divine energy. Living in union with Christ is the gift of *all* the elect. Virginity is the gift of some; it is a framework for this union.

ABOUT THE UNION THAT GIVES LIFE TO VIRGINITY

The union enframed by virginity is the common union of all Christians with the three divine Persons. The specific gift of virginity is a certain transparency of this union in our consciousness, an obscure experience of God's personal presence, which is so strong in its weakness that it calls a man away from human companionship and installs him in God's recreating friendship. No person could desire virginity, unless he found another person who is more lovable than any man.

The union with God takes place on a spiritual level; it is not a material communication. It strengthens the spirit of the human person who receives it, but in no way fulfills his natural desire to be one with a human companion. Yet, it makes the man whole, and the spiritual abundance that he receives reverberates in the body so much that there is a decreasing sense of frustration, and an increasing experience of fulfillment for the whole person. Natural instincts do not die, but they begin to learn to give way to new impulses that come from the Holy Spirit.

In other words, God gives a spiritual gift, but this gift is never transformed into a material medicine. The physical and psychological laws of human nature remain in operation; no miracle takes place.

An example will illustrate this point. When the Holy Spirit inspires a person to take up fasting for the sake of the kingdom, for some spiritual good, the Spirit does not promise that the person concerned will not be hungry; he will be. The Spirit is effectively pledging himself only to give a new spiritual strength that helps the one fasting to bear the hunger for some greater good. Moreover, the spiritual strength will balance the whole person, and may make him happy and relaxed even if hungry—provided the fasting remains within the limits of prudence.

Similarly, the spiritual union with God from which virginity originates does not fulfill the desires of the body, but the Holy Spirit lifts the whole man into another, spiritual world where the grace of God enriches even the body.

VIRGINITY IS AN ANTICIPATION OF THE GRACE OF RESURRECTION

With the resurrection of Christ and the coming of the Holy Spirit, God's glorious kingdom entered into our human history. With the dawn of the first Christian Easter, and with the day of the first Christian Pentecost, a new glorious age began, an age that God the Father has prepared from eternity, revealed through his Son, and perfected by the sending of his Spirit.

In this new age immortal glory and power are being distributed among the children of men through the Holy Spirit. Heaven meets earth, eternity joins time. The grace of virginity, as it springs from charity, belongs to this age.

Those who are baptized in Christ die with him in their baptism, and are raised from the dead in him. The glory and power of his resurrection is on them; it heals them, strengthens them, and makes them long for the manifestation of the glory of the children of God that is now hidden. The gift of virginity is a small share in the glory of the risen Christ. St. Paul says that the body of Christ was vivified by the Spirit; the resurrection consisted in the infusion of the strength of the Spirit into the inert body of Christ. The grace of virginity is the infusion of the strength of the Spirit into a mortal man, the infusion of a spiritual strength that makes the body more alive than it ever was, alive in a new spiritual kingdom. Virginity is the manifestation of the hidden glory of God's children.

Hence the transformation. Those who are virgins are anxious about the affairs of the Lord. The center of gravity in their lives lies in a new world, and from this arises a spiritual alertness of the whole person to the inspirations of the Spirit, a sensitivity to new light and fuller love. The eternal kingdom of God is present in this temporal world; but the divine gift is carried in a vessel of clay. This circumstance does not change the nature of the gift, but it should make the person who receives it cautious.

VIRGINITY IS A DYNAMIC VIRTUE

The gift of virginity could easily be conceived as a static, perfectly finished gift that, once given, endures forever, provided it is not willingly lost or destroyed. Nothing is further from the truth. The parable of the mustard seed applies to virginity as well as to any other Christian virtue. In the beginning it is a small seed: it needs the evangelical good soil to grow and to develop. As a young plant it is tender and sensitive: it needs help and protection, but when it grows into a large tree it can stand alone, it can weather the storm, and give shelter to many.

The dynamic character of the virtue of virginity is rooted in our union with the Trinity, which is not a static gift. Once given, it is there to develop steadily. The impact of God's presence on the life of a Christian should continuously deepen; the love of God that was infused into his heart should help him to grow into the full stature of Christ. Since virginity originates in this union, it has the same dynamic character.

The union of the virgin Mary with the Holy Spirit was perfect, therefore the strength of her virginity was perfect. A similar law applies to other human beings; the strength of their union with God is reflected in the strength of their virginity—if they receive this gift. No exception is possible; virginity cannot be stronger than the union.

It will be plain human good sense and Christian wisdom to draw the practical consequences. There are no two persons who are equally gifted and no two persons who are equally strong. Each one should honestly assess his gift, and live accordingly. When the good seed of virginity is sown in a human nature that is full of emotional turmoil and imbalances, the seed can easily be killed—Christ our Lord says so. The growing plant will need care and attention; if these are not given, the plant may perish. But what wise man would build a wall to protect a strong, fully grown tree? The tree should stand free so that the weary pilgrims on their way to the new Jerusalem can see it from afar, and find shelter under its strong branches.

The wisdom in preserving virginity lies in sensing and following the progress indicated by the Spirit. To seek too much human fulfillment while the gift of virginity is taking root may cut short a developing special friendship with God. The friends of God have always been trained and tested in some sort of desert; it may have been symbolic, it may have been spiritual, but desert it was. It can be bypassed only in the imagination of some, never in reality. Not even Christ bypassed it.

But when the gift of virginity develops, it is a light that must shine out, it is leaven that must be put into the mass in order to sanctify our world. Apart from particular and specialized vocations, therefore, virgins should meet the people of God and talk to them about the kingdom. They should announce the good news in a loud voice (the Gospel uses the expression, "from the rooftop"), and they should communicate their love and charity to every human being. Such biblical ideas should help with the problem of revising the law of enclosure or cloister or the involvement of consecrated persons in temporal affairs.

To hide one's light can be a sin against the Spirit. Some will ask, no doubt: is there not a danger that the light might sometimes be extinguished? There is such a danger and it can be taken for granted that some lights will be snuffed out by the darkness. However the solution is not to enclose all the lights behind strong walls and windshields, but to let even more lights shine out so that the world can see them as signs of God's presence among us.

The aim and purpose of consecrated virginity is to make the communication of God's love easier; virginity has meaning only "for the sake of the kingdom"—the Kingdom to be spread. To make the preaching and the teaching of the kingdom more difficult for those who are consecrated virgins would be to reverse the hierarchy of Christian values. It would mean to imprison the love of

God for the sake of precautions. Virginity, in ordinary circumstances, is given for the sake of better dedication to an apostolic task, for a better communication of graces.

THE APOSTOLIC FINALITY OF VIRGINITY

Every Christian is a disciple and an apostle of his Master. It follows that his union with Christ has to be deepened and communicated to others. It is in this communication that the apostolic finality of virginity comes to the fore, not in the simple and somewhat crude sense that a virgin has no family, and is therefore free in time and space to meet others, or in the sense only that he can be better dedicated. It is true that when there is a question of going to foreign missions or of serving persons afflicted with contagious diseases the celibate priest is in a better position than the married person. Yet the substance of the question is not there.

The substance lies in the intensity of God's love that can develop in a virgin, and can be communicated with a freedom that only virginity can give. This freedom is primarily internal: God's message flows through a human mind and heart and is not interfered with by our human ways of thinking and doing. The union given to a Christian is a dynamic gift; it has to be communicated—the kingdom has to expand. Virginity is the best vehicle for this expansion. It is thus that the saying of Christ about celibacy "on behalf of the kingdom" receives its full meaning; it includes the spreading of the kingdom.

Therefore, seclusion within a cloister or an enclosure remains a specific vocation: holy and legitimate, blessed and praised by the Church, but not the general rule. The common evangelical rule is that the virgin or the celibate has the vocation to facilitate the propagation of the kingdom. Any other interpretation would suffer from an internal contradiction. The cult of virginity is valid in the context of apostolic life; it is given to facilitate the communication of God's message. This is said with profound respect for those who have a different vocation, and serve God within the cloister. Their virginity fosters an intense prayer life through which they serve the kingdom. It is through prayer that the apostolic finality of virginity is fully present there.

COMMUNITY LIFE AND CONSECRATED VIRGINITY

It is natural that those who receive the special gift of virginity like to come together to form a community. Such a community itself should be marked by the virtue of virginity in its internal relations among the members and in its external relations with others.

Within the community, the gift of virginity should free each of the members from human anxieties and make him more able to spread the love of God. Personal communication should therefore be easier and more relaxed than in any other type of community. The purpose of the members should be to introduce each other into the mystery of the union with God. We come back to the same principle: the meaning of virginity is to increase the love of God and the expansion of it. Practical consequences abound. Overstressed silence can paralyze this communication, and so can the restrictive practices in matters of meetings and correspondence among the members of the same religious institute. Such practices run counter to the meaning God has given to virginity, which is to free the person, even externally in human relations, and not to build a wall around him. The way of life of a community should reflect the impact of the grace of virginity on that community, and should favor a delicate sensitivity to grace that is so characteristic of virginity. The community should have an integrity of mind and spirit in all common actions, an integrity that is a dedication to the inspirations of the Holy Spirit.

In short, the atmosphere in the community should favor an all-pervading union with God. Happiness and relaxation are of primary importance in creating a common disposition for God's grace. Strains and tensions are probably the most frequent impediments to God's work—even strains and tensions that are the result of common observance. The human faculties become paralyzed, unable to perceive God's graces, and still less able to sustain a loving attention to him. Man is a social being and cannot be anything else. By renouncing the close companionship in marriage, he does not slough off his social nature; therefore, he needs a happy and relaxed community life with all the freedom that virginity can add to it. If anything, the gift of virginity makes a person more social than he ever was: it opens him up to all.

The spirit of friendship is fostered in a good community. This statement is in accord with biblical thought and with Catholic tradition. Nowhere in the Bible is friendship condemned; it is praised in many places, and the history of the Church abounds in instances of great friendships. There cannot be a healthy relationship with God without a healthy relationship with human friends. In individual cases, however, the natural and supernatural resources of the individual should be taken into account.

If someone is strongly rooted in God's grace, friendship too becomes a source of grace. If one is not so rooted, the balance of natural instincts and supernatural gifts is precarious, and he may approach the best opportunity for friendship with a confused mind and unruly emotions. Each community, and each person in it, needs wisdom to know the limits of individual strength. Members of the community need guidance to protect themselves when necessary, and supernatural courage to discard unnecessary restrictions.

Friendship between consecrated persons can be best described as the friendship of travelers: they look and travel in the same direction. The friendship between a man and a woman which develops into marriage can be described as the friendship of dwellers: they look at each other. A sign of a good friendship is that it is not exclusive in spirit; on the contrary, it wants to expand. Friends are eager to share what they have with many others. The better friends they are, the less they are involved with each other; they are involved *together* in others.

The gift of virginity can be destroyed by overprotection. If, under the guise of protecting virginity, genuine and happy social relations are blocked, a person is deprived of one of his most basic human needs and rights, and a fundamental sense of frustration is bound to cause tension and unhappiness. This may lead to the conviction that he had no vocation to virginity, a false conclusion under the circumstances. However, since the frustration persists, a young man may leave the seminary, or a young woman may give up her religious vocation. The gift of virginity has been destroyed by misguided good will.

It does not follow in any way that sentimental and futile social relationships should be fostered: the goal is health, not a new type of illness. A community of consecrated persons must consider, also, what the right balance should be in its relationship with those who do not belong to the community. The greater the impact of grace on the community, and the closer its union with God, the less enclosure it will need; the less the community is rooted in union with God, the stricter the enclosure will have to be. It should be remarked, also, that the happier the community, the fewer the restrictions needed, because the internal happiness will anchor every person to the community, and will call him back when he is away from it. But it will take a multiplicity of rules to keep an unhappy community together, since all natural (and even supernatural) forces will pull individuals away from it.

LAMP WITHOUT LIGHT

The essence of virginity is that it is a special means of achieving union with God; it protects, defends, and shelters this union. The tragedy that may occur in some who are consecrated virgins is that virginity is present but the union remains lifeless: there is no dynamic growth and development in it. The framework exists, but the content is too weak. Such a person is like a lamp that sheds no light; he leaves his surroundings in darkness.

This is a tragedy that *could* happen to a consecrated person. He may keep the integrity of heart and body, but at the same time his internal life will not know the light and love of the Holy Spirit. Frequently, he will take refuge in an extreme legalism. In such a case virginity is nearly meaningless and can not be called a true sign, for the essence of a sign is that it connects two persons or connects persons with different places and objects. An empty virginity does not connect anyone with eternal life; a lamp without oil cannot give light.

CONCLUSION

It is easier to see now why virginity has the primacy in religious consecration. Through virginity a special bond is established between God and man: they become companions. The grace of virginity is a spiritual grace, yet, it vivifies the body and gives a new balance to it. It is therefore the anticipation of the grace of resurrection, the manifestation of the otherwise hidden glory of the children of God. The other aspects of consecration follow virginity. A human person who has entered a new, glorious, and spiritual world through virginity will not want to be the slave of material and temporal things. He will vow freedom by professing poverty. He will also recognize the living Christ in the Church, and as a rule, he will ask for a deeper association with the visible Church by dedicating himself to works of charity in a religious community. In this way he will share the glory of the risen Christ, and he will do the saving work of the mortal Christ.

3

Possession of the Kingdom: Poverty

"How happy are the poor in spirit; theirs is the kingdom of heaven" (Mt 5,3) . This text is very difficult to interpret in English so as to catch the original thought. The original Hebrew or Aramaic our Lord used has no strict correspondence in Greek, the inspired text of the New Testament; second, the Greek is not easily translated into English. The French found an expression that is fairly near to the original: "How happy are those who have *une âme pauvre.*" A literal English translation, however, "How happy are those who have a poor soul," would destroy the full meaning of the words of our Lord; but the usual translation, "Blessed are the poor in spirit," does not yield the full significance either.

This chapter is simply an attempt to explain what it means to be poor in spirit, or to have a poor soul. The essence of the virtue of poverty, and in particular of religious poverty, lies precisely in this poverty of heart.

THE BIBLICAL BACKGROUND

When our Lord said in the Sermon on the Mount "How happy are the poor in spirit," or "those who have a poor soul," or are "poor of heart," for "theirs is the kingdom of heaven," he was echoing a long tradition of Israel. The poor of Yahweh, or the poor, meek, and humble people who trusted and loved God, formed a class apart in the history of Israel. They were God's chosen ones, the heirs of God's promises to Abraham and his posterity, although they were frequently oppressed by the rich and powerful.

The developed concept of poverty in the Old Testament meant a religious disposition, a genuine devotion towards God, much more than physical deprivation. It is true that, in the beginning, when "Israel was a child," poverty was equated with disgrace and wealth with God's favor. If a person was poor, it was a sign that he was not loved by God; and if he was rich and prosperous, it meant that God loved him. This, however, was a primitive idea, and we find a strong reaction against it in the Book of Job. Israel outgrew this idea, and gradually a new conception began to dawn on it, which later entered into the official prayer of the Church. To this day we pray in the divine office: "Divitias et paupertatem ne dederis mihi sed victui meo tribuas necessaria"—"Lord, do not give me wealth and do not lead me into misery either, but do give me what is necessary for my life."

Nevertheless, in spite of the conception that the ideal condition lies in a proper balance between riches and misery, the laws of social justice were not always observed in Israel. There were many poor people, and frequently they were poor because of the unjust behavior of the rich and powerful. No wonder the Hebrews asked: Why is it that so many good men have to live in poverty, being oppressed by the rich? How can the justice of God allow it? The prophets answered these questions and rose to defend the poor and the unjustly persecuted. They declared that the poor are protected by Yahweh, the God of Israel, and that one day God will come and give justice to them.

There are some strong passages in the Book of Amos against the rich who exploited the poor. Amos was a shepherd, and what we would call today an agricultural laborer. One day he received an order from Yahweh to go and prophesy to the people of Israel:

> I was no prophet, neither did I belong to any of the brotherhoods of prophets, . . . I was a shepherd, and looked after sycamores: but it was Yahweh who took me from herding the flock, and Yahweh who said, "Go, prophesy to my people Israel" (Am 7, 14–15).

Much of Amos' preaching was concerned with widespread social injustices, and he did not mince words when he had to denounce crying abuses. He spoke of God's judgment against the rich women of Samaria:

> Listen to this word, you cows of Bashan living in the mountain of Samaria, oppressing the needy, crushing the poor, saying to your husbands, 'Bring us something to drink!' The Lord Yahweh swears this by his holiness: The days are coming to you now when you will be dragged out with hooks, the very last of you with prongs. Out you will go, each by the nearest breach in the wall, to be driven all the way to Hermon. It is Yahweh who speaks (Am 4, 1–3).

The prophet's words reflect the conception that God protects the poor and the little people in Israel and that he will punish their rich oppressors.

> Listen to this, you who trample on the needy and try to suppress the poor people of the country, you who say, 'When will New Moon be over so that we can sell our corn, and sabbath, so that we can market our wheat? Then by lowering the bushel, raising the shekel, by

swindling and tampering with the scales, we can buy up the poor for money, and the needy for a pair of sandals, and get a price even for the sweepings of the wheat.' Yahweh swears it by the pride of Jacob, 'Never will I forget a single thing you have done.' Is this not the reason for the earthquakes, for its inhabitants all mourning, and all of it heaving, like the Nile, then subsiding, like the river of Egypt?

'That day—it is the Lord Yahweh who speaks—I will make the sun go down at noon, and darken the earth in broad daylight. I am going to turn your feasts into funerals, all your singing into lamentation; I will have your loins all in sackcloth, your heads all shaved. I will make it a mourning like the mourning for an only son, as long as it lasts it will be like a day of bitterness (Am 8, 4–10).

The same thought emerges in the words of Jeremiah. His was the duty to announce doomsday for Israel. Nobody liked to listen to him, quite obviously, and so they mocked and rejected him. He was so depressed that he reproached Yahweh for having chosen him to be a prophet:

You have seduced me, Yahweh, and I have let myself be seduced; you have overpowered me: you were the stronger. I am a daily laughing-stock, everybody's butt. Each time I speak the word, I have to howl and proclaim: 'Violence and ruin!' The word of Yahweh has meant for me insult, derision, all day long (Jer 20, 7–8).

This is the prayer of a poor man who is worn out by the burden of his office, oppressed and persecuted from all sides:

I used to say, 'I will not think about him, I will not speak in his name any more'. Then there seemed to be a fire burning in my heart, imprisoned in my bones. The effort to restrain it wearied me, I could not bear it. I hear so many disparaging me, ' "Terror from every side!" De-

nounce him! Let us denounce him!' All those who used
to be my friends watched for my downfall, 'Perhaps he
will be seduced into error. Then we will master him and
take our revenge! ' (Jer 20, 9–10).

But God will protect the poor man:

> But Yahweh is at my side, a mighty hero; my opponents
> will stumble, mastered, confounded by their failure; ever-
> lasting, unforgettable disgrace will be theirs. But you,
> Yahweh Sabaoth, you who probe with justice, who scru-
> tinise the loins and heart, let me see the vengeance you
> will take on them, for I have committed my cause to you
> (Jer 20, 11–12).

Jermiah was secure, because he was protected by God.

From this conception that God protects the poor, the
belief emerged that the poor are the chosen ones of God.
At the same time, the very concept of poverty underwent a
transformation. Instead of meaning only deprivation, frustration, misery, it took on a new significance which
connoted spiritual riches. To be poor and good of heart
meant to be loved by God, it meant a right to be protected
by Yahweh, although in a mysterious way. The word
poverty took on a religious cast, and the poor ones of Yahweh began to form a particular group in Israel. Consciously or unconsciously they felt that they belonged to
God and God belonged to them: they *were* the chosen
people of God. If many in Israel did not live up to this
ideal, there remained everywhere a faithful group of persons who respected the law and waited for the redemption
of Israel. They were rarely rich; they were the poor ones of
Yahweh. They were the small ones, the little ones, who
were more than once oppressed, to whom justice was not
always given, but who belonged to God and waited to see

the justice of God and to experience the grace of redemption. Gradually, one could say, a particular liturgy of the poor developed in the Psalms; Psalm 131 is an example:

> O Lord, my heart is not proud
> nor haughty my eyes.
> I have not gone after things too great
> nor marvels beyond me.
>
> Truly I have set my soul
> in silence and peace.
> A weaned child on its mother's breast,
> even so is my soul.
>
> O Israel, hope in the Lord
> both now and for ever (*Grail Breviary Psalter*).

This is the prayer of the poor. There are many similar supplications in the Psalms. A large number of them are simply the prayer of the persecuted poor; their spirituality is expressed in the liturgical songs of Israel. The enemies of the poor were the proud, conceited, and godless persons.

To sum up: poverty acquired a religious sense that implied not just physical deprivation, not just sheer physical misery, but a title and a right to God's love. In fact, when the Hebrew texts of the Old Testament were translated into Greek by the Jews themselves, the Greek word *praus* was used for the *poor* of the Hebrew. *Praus* designated not just a person living in misery, but rather one who was of meek, gentle, peaceful, or humble disposition. The translators knew the religious meaning of the Hebrew word *poor;* and when they searched for a Greek word to render it, they did not choose a term that meant physical poverty only, but one that expressed the internal disposition of a good, simple, humble, and peaceful person.

By the time of our Lord, the theology of this religious

poverty had reached great maturity. The poor of Israel considered themselves the friends of God, his beloved ones. They remained faithful to Yahweh; they were the *remnant* of Israel, the small group that did not betray God's trust. The promises were for them. The finest expression of their spirit flowers in the Magnificat:

> He has shown the power of his arm, he has routed the proud of heart . . . and exalted the lowly. The hungry he has filled with good things, the rich sent empty away (Lk 1, 51–53).

Our Lady's hymn is nothing else than an echo of the prayer of the poor of Yahweh: God exalted the humble and dethroned the rich; God enriched the poor and made the wealthy miserable.

Our Lady and St. Joseph, and later the apostles, all belonged to this remnant of Israel, to the small group who remained faithful to Yahweh. They were poor even physically, but they were rich spiritually. In fact, Christ showed a preference for them: he chose a humble virgin from the house of David to be his Mother; he chose a young carpenter to protect her, and when the Messiah was born, shepherds were the first to bring him their love and homage.

When our Lord wanted to choose the twelve pillars of his future Church, the apostles, he chose them from among the poor of Israel. They were poor of heart, they expected the redemption of Israel. They were not chosen because they were poor in worldly goods—they may have been in their own way fairly well-to-do, but they were poor in this full religious sense of the term. They were the faithful ones, the ones who observed the law and put their hope in God. They had a genuine goodness in their soul. They did not have much education in the formal sense of the term.

They were simple people: sometimes they quarreled among themselves as people do; but they were loved by God and they loved him.

Let us first consider what can be called the positive side of the virtue of poverty and then its negative aspect, although it is hardly correct to divide poverty into positive and negative elements. Its reality is one and indivisible; if we distinguish two aspects of it, we do so only to consider poverty in an orderly fashion.

A PREVIOUS CONDITION TO POVERTY: THE EXPERIENCE OF
THE KINGDOM OF GOD

Our Lord says: "How happy are the poor in spirit [the poor of heart]; theirs is the kingdom of heaven." He does not say that the kingdom of God *will be* theirs. This actual possession of the kingdom of God and the experience of its possession is really the key to evangelical poverty in general and to a life of poverty in a religious institute.

We cannot be poor in the religious sense of the term unless we are already in the possession of the kingdom of God. Therefore, our attention should be first directed towards this possession; once we have it and its reality is experienced, then we shall be able to lead a poor life in the evangelical sense of the term. Our poverty will be in proportion to our possession of the kingdom of God.

In other words, in order to be poor with Christ, it is necessary to have some experience of the riches of Christ. Unless a person experiences these riches, he cannot and *will not* be poor. This is not to say that he could not lead a life of deprivation—he could; nor that he could not lead a life of extreme austerity—he could; but this of itself would not be genuine poverty in the biblical sense of the term. In order to be poor with Christ and in order to enjoy poverty with Christ, the experience of God's kingdom is necessary. Without it, poverty would somehow be distorted, or at least, it would be a soulless poverty.

But what does this experience of the riches of God mean? It means what it says: my whole soul and even my body must know that there is a God and that God loves me and that there is friendship between God and me. There should be a deep conviction that God has found me in this world and has invited me to enter his kingdom. There must be, in a good sense, in a sober sense, a happy realization that I have found the Messias. Then my attention will turn to Christ and away from the world. I will want to be with him and I shall not be covetous of the riches of this world. There will be an internal transformation; a slow and gradual transformation, no doubt, over many years. Even for twenty years, perhaps, we are just beginners. But beginner or not, a person who has experienced the presence of the kingdom of God will be able to practice something of the poverty of Christ. No one can follow Christ who has not met him; the experience of his presence is the previous condition of following him and sharing his poor way of life. No religious can live his own life fully, unless he has experienced God's presence in this world; the experience may be obscure but it will be real.

From the experience of this presence, there will follow an attraction towards God. God will draw me towards himself; he will try to seduce me as he did Jeremiah: "You have seduced me, Yahweh, and I have let myself be seduced; you have overpowered me: you were the stronger" (Jer 20, 7). This is what happens to nearly every person in the beginning of his conversion to God. God treats him like a child and attracts him with sweetness; the person is literally enticed to follow God. One day, however, he will wake from this dream life, the day when God begins to give him stronger food. This day may well come during the novitiate in the case of a religious. But it is through the experience of his goodness that God is able to entice us to serve him.

It is correct to say, then, that even the beginnings of our religious life are rooted in the presence of God, the attraction of God, the love of God. It is precisely this experience that awakens love in me and makes me turn to God. It all may be a very long process; it rarely happens abruptly, but may extend for ten, twenty, or thirty years, or for our whole life. This is important to keep in mind.

When this love is experienced, even in a small way, the person *is* already in possession of the kingdom of God. He has found the Messias. His whole humanity, his soul, and even his body experiences somehow the presence of God and the love of God, and the need in himself to answer this love. He will therefore be able to turn away from the created world and to turn towards God. This is not the end of the process, however, because one day (day meaning years here) this love will expand. One's attention has been centered on the beloved Person, on God; now one will notice that really the whole created universe is nothing else than the incarnation of the beauty of God. Then he will notice the riches of God in this created world; then he will come back to the world and love it precisely because everything in it speaks to him about God. A short passage from St. John of the Cross illustrates how a soul immersed in God finds him in all created things:

My Beloved:
  The mountains,
  The solitary wooded valleys,
  The strange islands,
  The sonorous rivers,
  The whisper of the breezes,
  The tranquil night,
  The time of the rising of the dawn,
  The silent music,
  The sounding solitude,
  The supper that recreates and enkindles love
                              (*Spiritual Canticles*, XIII).

Everything, the whole creation, the mountains and the valleys and the supper, that usual supper that we take in our community—they all speak about the beloved One. In St. John, that sense of finding God everywhere was highly developed; but there is no reason why we could not have a small spark, at least, of that perfection, and notice the beauty of God, say, in at least some suppers that we share.

St. Francis of Assisi, too, in his poverty, found God in all things:

Be praised, my Lord, of all your creature world,
And first of all Sir Brother Sun,
Who brings the day, and light you give to us through him,
And beautiful is he, agleam with mighty splendor:
Of you, Most High, he gives us indication.

Be praised, my Lord, through Sisters Moon and Stars,
In the heavens you have formed them,
bright and fair and precious.

. . . .
Be praised, my Lord, through Sister Water,
For greatly useful, lowly, precious, chaste is she.

Be praised, my Lord, through Brother Fire,
Through whom you brighten up the night,
And fair is he, and gay, and vigorous, and strong.

Be praised, O Lord, through our sister Mother Earth,
For she sustains and guides our life,
and yields us divers fruits, with tinted flowers, and grass
(Canticle of Brother Sun).

Only a person of "poor heart" can possess the universe in such a supreme degree. St. John of the Cross, St. Francis of Assisi, and many others experienced the kingdom of God in themselves and the presence of God in the whole universe. Therefore their poverty reached the highest perfection. The lesson for us is that unless we have some experience of the love of God, we cannot reach any kind of perfection in the matter of poverty.

Incidentally, perhaps it is not out of place to note that, while so much is being said today about poverty in the Church, this previous condition is frequently forgotten. No wonder many attempts to reform simply do not work. One cannot become poor overnight; one must be rich first. Unless one is rich in God and with God, one cannot be poor in this world. God made us in such a way that we cannot love in a vacuum; we cannot leave the world behind and have nothing. We must first find God and his kingdom, and then we shall be able to renounce earthly possessions and become poor. Then we shall have other riches to lean on and to live on. If the Church ought to become poorer (and in some way there is no doubt that it ought), in some other way it ought to become richer—if the Church ought to become poorer, the previous condition for it is that it should become richer in the love of God. Then a greater poverty will be possible, but not otherwise. If those who represent the Church grow in the love of God, they will grow in evangelical poverty too; if the previous condition is not there, no physical poverty and deprivation will last long, and any attempt to increase it will collapse.

So poverty begins by an experience of God's kingdom. One cannot insist enough on this aspect. The lack of this experience is perhaps the reason why many try to resist the *aggiornamento* today. They did not experience the movement of the Holy Spirit. It would be useless to impose new rules on them: we have to help them first to recognize the work of the Spirit in the events. Once they experience the presence of the Spirit in this movement of renewal, the *aggiornamento* will come quite easily; but if we try to push people into some sort of *aggiornamento* which is merely external, first they will resist, and if they do not succeed in resisting, they will cooperate meanly and grudgingly, which means ineffectively. It will not be a work of love. After a year or two, they will show that the new ideas are simply inapplicable in practice, and therefore we have to go back to the state of things as they were before. The frustration of an inspiration of the Spirit will be completed.

Perhaps it is well to remark that we have to consider the work of Vatican II in the context of the whole tradition of the Church. The Council's intention was not to speak explicitly and at length about the deepest friendship that a human person can have with the divine Persons. This was taken for granted because it is so much in the tradition of the Church, but the Council certainly intended to build all the reforms on this friendship, and, therefore, if we want to talk about *aggiornamento* it is well to begin with the question: How can we deepen our friendship with God, today, in the particular circumstances of the twentieth century? This question must be faced and answered by every individual, every community. Once the answer to this preliminary question is honestly attempted, then it will be easier to carry out the practical injunctions of the Council. Everything will fall into its own place, if the hierarchy of values is preserved.

The person who has established this friendship with God, who has become rich in God while enjoying this friendship, will turn to the world, too, for the whole world is the incarnation of God's love. In the world he will notice above all the human persons, hungry for God, and perhaps unconsciously waiting for his kingdom. That is why apostolic work, in one way or another, follows prayer. Anyone who is a friend of God will be a friend of man. We spoke before of St. Teresa who insisted so much on solitude and the necessity of remaining within the cloister, and yet who cheerfully went out so many times to establish new foundations. It was the Holy Spirit who brought this about, perhaps without St. Teresa's full realization of how she was being directed; apostolic activity followed her prayer—and nourished it, of course. The example of Benedictines and other monks also is pertinent: they took a vow of stability, a vow to remain in the same place and, nevertheless, they converted the greater part of Europe to Christianity. The fruit of their prayer overflowed into apostolic work. Perhaps none among Christian writers, even among the inspired authors of the biblical books, expressed more strikingly than Saint Paul how this close friendship with God leads to an overwhelming love of man. Paul's statement is so strong that we could easily consider it a paradox, but he did not intend it in that way. The love of man is stronger in him than the desire to see and enjoy the glory of Christ immediately:

Life to me, of course, is Christ, but then death would
bring me something more; but then again, if living in
this body means doing work which is having good results
—I do not know what I should choose. I am caught in
this dilemma: I want to be gone and be with Christ,
which would be very much the better, but for me to stay
alive in this body is a more urgent need for your sake.
This weighs with me so much that I feel sure I shall sur-
vive and stay with you all, and help you to progress in
the faith and even increase your joy in it; and so you will
have another reason to give praise to Christ Jesus on my
account when I am with you again (Phil 1, 21–26).

POVERTY OF HEART MEANS TO LIVE ON GIFTS

Let us give a more detailed description of this "poor soul,"
or the soul of a poor man, who is possessed by God and
who is in possession of God. When one speaks about such a
soul, one does not necessarily mean a perfect person.
"Good Christian" is not synonymous with "perfect person"; good Christian is synonymous with a person who is
loved by God, and who receives this love. It is God's mystery that he loves, and deeply loves, imperfect persons.

Who then is a person who is "poor in his heart?" The
answer is that a poor person is one who lives on gifts, and
gives away what he has. He relies on the goodness of others, but he does not make a collection of the gifts received.
This twofold aspect—to receive and to give—really expresses one idea: the idea of religious poverty. We think of
St. Francis of Assisi who begged for alms and gave away all
that he had. Those two gestures are the expression of the
same poor person; the disposition of his whole soul is
there.

A poor person lives on gifts, and to be a Christian is to
be a poor person. The kingdom of God is a gift from God

and a poor soul clings to God, because he knows that without him, he would fall immediately. If he is able to remain within the kingdom of God it is because God gives him strength, literally holds him in his hand. We are all living on the mercy of God.

Further, a Christian has to be understanding: it is the privilege of a poor man to understand other people's misery. If one is living on gifts, one should never despise a person who has not received the same gifts. A Christian who despises a sinner, is unfriendly to a sinner, is harsh on a sinner, is a poor man who is harsh on his fellow-poor: the worst kind of conceit.

To be poor, therefore, means to live on gifts. Anyone who wishes to know if he is poor of heart, should ask if he is conscious of his needs, supernatural and natural, and if he is ready to extend his hand every day for gifts and for help. Is he open to advice, to admonition, to help from others? Real poverty is there. He might be saving huge sums for his institute, but he is really a poor religious if he has not got a poor soul and his whole being is not open all day long to receive gifts from others, like a poor man who receives gifts from the rich, from the other poor ones, from grown-ups, and from children.

POVERTY OF HEART MEANS TO GIVE

Poverty of heart means also to give away what we have. This is the other gesture of St. Francis of Assisi, and in fact, we find the same gesture all through the history of the Church: the gesture of good Christians who are poor of heart; they gave away their possessions.

Here we touch the heart of the matter. It is important to be able to receive; but it is still more important to be able to give. And the best we can give is ourselves. Few of us are able to give away money, few of us are able to distribute material things; at any rate, religious superiors would not always like it. But any religious, and religious under any discipline, has the capacity to give himself. Real poverty of heart lies in this: one does not belong to one's self—one belongs to God, to the Church, and to every child of God in the Church, and to every human being on earth. No doubt, we all experience the temptation to keep what we have, and we fail many times in this internal poverty, because we are rich and want to stay rich without ever realizing it.

The soul of poverty lies in giving myself away. To begin with small things, because our life is composed of small things, it means not to be covetous about myself. I should not covet my own time, but I should want to give it. This is hard: I have my own timetable, my own program, my own dream-castle to be built within two years. Everything for it is worked out, and now come X and Y, asking for help, and interfering with my plans. I have to choose between building that castle and helping a child of God. If I am kept busy by the Church for a greater interest, by all means, I should fulfill the wishes of the Church, but this is extremely rare. Most of the time, the will of God would be that I should be poor for God's sake: I should let other people disrupt my time-table, undo my plans, and destroy my dream-castle. This is real poverty— and to do it in such a way that people will not even notice makes it poverty that is all the more real. Let others appeal to me, and let them take it for granted that unless I am held back by obedience, or by what is a genuinely more important task (I will have to make a responsible judgement), I am going to help them. Let it be known that what is most important to me are the children of God, and not a business, not a thing to be done. Human persons should hold my interest above all, persons who need help and understanding, because nothing is so perfect in the kingdom of God as a person. When the providence of God brings me a person, the will of God will normally be that I should help the person, and, if you like, "waste my time" on him. It may be a temptation to concentrate too much on a business and too little on the person concerned. The logical answer to a question does not always solve the difficulty of the person who feels the weight of the problem. It may well be that what he needs is not a logical solution, but support and understanding. A poor man will be able to give his time in listening. Personal help sometimes consists in listening to another for an hour. By the end of the hour all the problems may have vanished. Your interlocutor may even tell you how marvelous you are in resolving problems, when perhaps you did not say more than a yes or no at appropriate places.

This giving of myself to another person is genuine poverty. It is the distributing of myself and letting other people take me. It is clear, however, that there ought to be a balance in this process of giving myself away: one has duties that must be done and must have priority. But the giving springs from an attitude of heart: if this poverty of heart is real, my duty will not suffer and at the same time a great deal of help will be given to others. This is exactly Our Lord's attitude:

> He went round the whole of Galilee teaching in their synagogues, proclaiming the Good News of the kingdom and curing all kinds of diseases and sickness among the people. His fame spread throughout Syria, and those who were suffering from diseases and painful complaints of

one kind or another, the possessed, epileptics, the paralysed, were all brought to him, and he cured them (Mt 4, 23–4).

Jesus made a tour through all the towns and villages, teaching in their synagogues, proclaiming the Good News of the kingdom and curing all kinds of diseases and sickness (Mt 9, 35).

This is what St. Paul did: he was Jew with the Jews and Greek with the Greeks, giving himself to the service of the Gospel and God's people:

Constantly travelling, I have been in danger from rivers and in danger from brigands, in danger from my own people and in danger from pagans; in danger in the towns, in danger in the open country, danger at sea and danger from so-called brothers. I have worked and laboured, often without sleep; I have been hungry and thirsty and often starving; I have been in the cold without clothes. And, to leave out much more, there is my daily preoccupation: my anxiety for all the churches. When any man has had scruples, I have had scruples with him; when any man is made to fall, I am tortured (2 Cor 11, 26–9).

Poverty of heart excludes any internal covetousness. A religious can become covetous in his heart more easily than he thinks. He can become possessive internally, and for the essence of poverty it does not make much difference whether he possesses a dreamcastle or a real one. If he is attached to either, he is no longer a poor man—the Gospel has not penetrated into his heart.

EXTERNAL POVERTY MEANS SACRIFICE

Those who are prepared to give themselves to others—to God, to the Church, and to their fellow men—are poor of heart. Because they enjoy this internal substance of poverty, they will not find it difficult to practice it externally. Rather, they will want to express their internal disposition in tangible, external deeds. Since they are poor of heart, they will seek to be poor materially. They will find also the right balance in the practice of material poverty.

It is in external expression that the poverty of consecrated religious is different from the poverty of a dedicated Christian. Internally there cannot be any difference, since poverty of heart is the reverse side of the possession of the kingdom; and this possession is for all Christians, as the Sermon on the Mount is for all Christians. Externally, however, a religious renounces his right or legal power over earthly possessions—a renouncement which could better be called a declaration of freedom. Since he is in possession of the kingdom, and of the earth *in God*, it would restrict his freedom to create particular legal relations with all the duties and worries involved. He already has more than that, and since he can avoid involvement with problems of ownership and administration of goods, he chooses to do so. This frees him in a singular way for the service of the Church; he can follow Christ with the ease and the liberty of the apostles who put down their nets and became disciples and companions of Jesus.

Apart from, and above this radical renunciation, external poverty will, to a large extent, be a question of such balance, and it will vary from one religious institute to another. This is so because it is the temporal, material expression of an internal spiritual disposition, and this external expression may vary according to different circumstances. There will always be an element of abnegation and mortification in it; at the same time, it will include an element of freedom. It will be marked by the cross of

Christ and by the liberty of his Spirit. External poverty will be a blend of genuine abnegation and mortification in the use of created things, and of genuine freedom in using anything, absolutely anything, that is necessary or helpful for the propagation of the Gospel. This element of abnegation and mortification was present in the life of Christ, but it was not the same all the time. For long years, when our Lord was with his Mother and foster-father in Nazareth, the Holy Family led a settled life. It was not an easy life; but there is no reason to think that it was a life of misery. We may assume that their life corresponded to the prayer: "Lord, do not lead me into misery; but do not give me riches either. Give me all that is necessary to sustain my life." This is what the Holy Family had: a modest way of life that at the same time did not crowd their days with material worries to such an extent that they had no leisure to praise God and enjoy his creation.

Many of the contemplative orders instinctively imitated the way of life of the Holy Family. The Carthusian who has a small house for himself, with four little rooms and a garden (when after all, strictly speaking, he could do with one room), is doing nothing else than putting into practice this very modest and austere, and still very human way of life of the Holy Family. If a religious institute wants to lead this kind of life, it certainly remains within the limits of the perfection of Christian poverty. It would be very unwise to go into a Carthusian monastery to preach to the monks that they should live four in one house instead of one living in a house with four little cells. The wisdom of the Spirit helped those monks to find their own way of life and the wisdom of the Church approved it; their choice should be respected by all.

But Christ our Lord knew greater poverty, too, espe-

cially during his public life; we should not, however, think
that his public life was always one of extreme misery. The
holy women who were so much in the background, but
came to the fore now and again, took care of him and his
apostles, whenever they could.

> Now after this he made his way through towns and
> villages preaching, and proclaiming the Good News of
> the kingdom of God. With him went the Twelve, as well
> as certain women who had been cured of evil spirits and
> ailments: Mary surnamed the Magdalene, from whom
> seven demons had gone out, Joanna the wife of Herod's
> steward Chuza, Susanna, and several others who provided
> for them out of their own resources (Lk 8, 1–3).

At the same time our Lord himself said: "Foxes have holes,
and the birds of the air have nests, but the Son of man has
nowhere to lay his head" (Mt 8, 20). He knew by experience the life of the poor.

Some religious institutes have as their purpose to follow Christ in his great apostolic poverty. This is God's
particular grace for them and they should not be disturbed
in following their vocation. The way of life of each institute should be respected and none should try to impose his
own grace and vocation on others. All should be poor of
heart, all should express this internal poverty in an effective and external way, but there will be a certain variey in
this external poverty, and that is how it should be. External poverty for a Carthusian will, perhaps, consist of silence, solitude, and fasting. For the member of an active
religious order, it will be, perhaps, in the work he is
doing: he may not be fasting, but he will have only fifteen
minutes for lunch because the next appointment is due.
He takes his food and he gives himself away. This type of
poverty is holy, too, and no one should belittle it.

This is why it is very unfair to preach the same type of poverty for the whole Church—God never wanted it. It would, however, be wrong again not to preach this element of mortification—both God and the Church want it. Religious poverty is a sacrifice offered to God; the cross of Christ is present in it. But we should not fully equate external poverty with the lack of material means; a priest who has an ordered house and a good library, but who gives his time, his whole person, all that he has to the service of God's people, may be much poorer, even externally, than another person who lives among bare walls and without a book, but is not easily available when his service is needed.

Without the element of sacrifice there cannot be true religious poverty. The offering of this sacrifice should be manifest in the life of the community, as well as in the life of the individual. In the life of the community—the mind of the Church is absolutely clear on this point—we should strive for the ideal that all material things in our possession should somehow reflect the poverty of Christ. This is a general rule, not easy to apply to particular cases; but the greatest of universities, the most efficient of schools or hospitals, should somehow show that they are under the management of God's poor ones. Nonetheless, poverty should never be at the expense of apostolic efficiency. Admittedly, it is difficult to find the right balance between these seemingly conflicting claims, but, with the help of the Holy Spirit, the balance can be found. Those who come into religious houses should feel a Christian atmosphere in the use of material things. There should be a difference between the buildings of religious, and secular buildings. Our external installations should reflect something of Christ's poverty without destroying high-quality service.

The community should witness to this Christian poverty in its social relations as well. Its members should have a universal friendship for God's children. If all the friends of a religious community are among the rich and wealthy of the town, can one really say that the community bears witness to the value of religious poverty? Obviously we should not exclude the rich from our apostolate—they may be much poorer than the poor—but at the same time, we should prove our love towards the poor by giving him the most precious gift, the gift of human friendship. If our friends are the rich only, would we not feel ourselves out of place in the company of the apostles? If we would, our hearts are not like the heart of Christ who felt very much at home with them.

This element of sacrifice should be present in the life of the individual religious, too, but the individual should decide its mode and extent, within the framework of the rule. The concrete solutions will vary much from one place to another, from one individual to another. There should be real poverty in the matter of food and clothing, but in a balanced way. In the matter of external poverty the main emphasis should remain on giving oneself to others. The complete picture of external poverty has not yet, however, been filled in.

EXTERNAL POVERTY IMPLIES THE USE OF CREATED THINGS

The external aspect of poverty includes, also, the use of material things for the kingdom of God. Only a poor person has the courage and determination to reach out for anything and to use it for the propagation of the Gospel. He knows that created things belong, in the final analysis, to no one but God, and therefore he is not too much worried about them. A poor person possesses the whole world; he moves about in it freely and with a certain independence and detachment. He has the courage, the determination, and the daring to start new things in the service of God. He has the courage even to take risks—an act that borders on the perfection of poverty—if for God's sake it is reasonable that a risk should be taken. Whatever the outcome, nothing will be lost because everything belongs to God and not to us. If, in spite of all care on his part, the enterprise does not succeed, he will not be unduly upset. If money invested, for instance, is lost despite all prudent care, it was lost in God's service, a service that includes calculated risks that sometimes end in failure.

Daring and courage in using created things are essential for true poverty. The story of St. Francis Xavier's first entry into Japan may serve as an illustration of this principle. When he first arrived in Japan he tried to preach the Gospel in a poor man's garb. Nobody listened to him, and he even became an object of mockery. Seeing his lack of success, he tried another method. He went back to the ship that had brought him and asked the captain to get him a fine suit of clothes, and any gift that he could spare. Then he sent a letter to the nearest of the Japanese potentates saying that the legate of the Pope had arrived, and would like to pay a state visit. He was received with honors. The first step in the evangelization of Japan was made by using created things, and not by being deprived of them.

The history of the Chinese missions provides another example. Missionaries could not penetrate into China as poor men; they were jailed or expelled without delay. When the Jesuits succeeded in entering, they were admitted as astronomers, rich in science and instruments, poor in their hearts. Their success as scientists was great, and soon they were making converts as well. Several of these missionaries held high positions as scientists at the court of the emperor. Their converts were among the higher classes, not because they wanted to limit their apostolate to them, but for the greater good. The structure of Chinese society was such that unless the educated classes received the Gospel, the ordinary people would not have accepted it.

Nothing better illustrates the spirit of detachment of these first missionaries in China than the fact that they asked for, and received from the Holy See, permission to have all liturgical services in Chinese. Only men of poor heart could have been able to make such a request, and abandon all the external expressions of piety they had known from childhood—for the sake of the Chinese.

Our duty is to do things in the best way we can think of, using all the means God has made available to us. A poor person possesses not only the kingdom of God but the whole material world. He has the courage to use material things for the sake of the Gospel. Perhaps one of the reasons why we were left so far behind in such matters as the use of radio, cinema, and television in apostolic work was that we did not have the right concept of poverty. We did not look on these inventions as instruments to convey the riches and beauty of God. Therefore, we did not concern ourselves about them—at least not to a very large extent. Sometimes well-meaning Catholics did even worse: they blamed those who were using and enjoying these means of communication, as if these instruments had been invented by the devil, and not conceived in the mind of God, in the Logos, the Son of God. Now the trend is changing; as the meaning of the Incarnation becomes clearer, we understand that we should not cut ourselves off from anything, because our vocation is to sanctify everything. But, in all honesty, we are still remarkably inefficient in the practice of this divine truth.

Poverty requires, also, the use of personal gifts in the service of God. It is depressing to see how sometimes in a religious house great care will be taken of material possessions, such as a car or television set, while human persons are neglected under the pretext of poverty. The gifts and talents that God has given them are not properly used, and as a result, God's kingdom suffers. God is not that much interested in motor cars, but he is supremely interested in his own children. The gifts God gives a person—gifts of grace, gifts of nature—should all be received with gratitude by the whole institute and used in the spirit of poverty, for the good of the Church.

In our work (including the work of internal administration), there should be greater efficiency. Our conception and practice of poverty is still far from being fully balanced. We train novices to use books gently, and save pieces of paper (and no master of novices should be blamed for this, because without external poverty it is difficult to become poor at heart), but an equal stress should be put on using all things with great freedom for the glory of God. If a journey to another country helps a person to become more creative in his work, superiors should help him to undertake the journey—provided it is not against the constitutions. Dangers lurk in this concept of poverty, to be sure, but all good things and truth itself are dangerous if they fall into the hands of those who abuse them. We should never discard something good, simply because it is dangerous; the danger should be removed, and full scope given to what is good.

If a man is a painter, for instance, and joins an apostolic institute in which his talent can be developed, it is reasonable that he should have a beautiful view that will inspire him. If he decided to join the Carthusians, he should not complain that the view is walled up. In both cases, however, he would remain faithful to the ideal of poverty.

This is precisely the point: we need external poverty, but we need still more the poverty that frees the heart from attachments and gives it the freedom of the children of God. If we do not have enough of external poverty (according to the vocation of each one) we do not have internal freedom.

To be enterprising and to have initiative frequently means to be ready to accept failure, to be prepared to burn one's fingers. Only a poor person is prepared for that. He can sacrifice everything for the sake of the Gospel because he has nothing. Yet, there is no person who enjoys this world so much (from time to time, at least) as he. He has *everything*.

CONCLUSION

It might be well to conclude by proposing an examination of conscience about true poverty in religious life: it may prove useful to all. Here are the questions: Is my first interest in the kingdom of God, or in other things? Do I try to find the experience of God's love first, and do I build my religious poverty on this experience?

Then: Have I accepted God's invitation to turn away from the world, and to turn towards him? And when I found him and was enriched by his friendship, did I in truth come back to the world, or have I remained in an artificial enclosure?

Again: Do I love the world? God loved the world, so much that he gave His only begotten Son for it. Unless I, too, love the world, I am not a poor man. Do I love all good things in this world, without discrimination? A poor religious loves every creature, animate or inanimate, but his love is never exclusive, and knows when an object should become a sacrifice. Divine love, which is Christian love, is never exclusive. The sign of selfish love is that it is exclusive: it is centered on an object, on a person; it is centered on a time-table, on a set way of life. Have I Christian love, or am I immersed in a selfish love?

The next question: Am I poor in my heart, that is, am I living on gifts? And to be practical about it: do I ever say I am shocked, do I ever say I would never do such and such? Do I ever ask how could so-and-so have done that? If I do, I am not a poor person in my heart; I am rich and in the worst way—I do not know that I am living on the mercy of God. Do I receive advice and help from others and do I ask for it? Am I able to carry on a dialog, which is an exchange of ideas between poor persons?

Furthermore: Am I prepared to give myself away, my person, my time, my program, my books—everything? Then, since poverty ought to be external, one should ask: Am I externally poor according to my own type of poverty? Is the element of sacrifice present in it? Is my external poverty a sign for my neighbors that the kingdom of God is here, with us?

In the use of this creation, do I have the freedom of the children of God? Am I efficient in the service of God? Have I the courage and the daring to take risks, even to the extent of accepting failure?

Such an examination of conscience should be extended to religious institutes themselves. Many of them are struggling with the problems of *aggiornamento,* the adaptation of their life to the new exigencies of the world, of the Church, and of the Holy Spirit. Some of these institutes will succeed in renewing themselves internally and externally. They will be blessed and they will know all the freshness of a second spring. Some others will not succeed. They will probably decline and know all the agonies of dying. It is not difficult to foretell that those institutes that are poor of heart will receive the grace of a renewal. They will be able to leave behind rules and customs suitable for a past age, but unnecessary or harmful today. These poor communities will be able to think afresh and make a new start, trusting God and not their possessions. They will be like the apostles who were able to leave behind their nets and families for Christ—the new Prophet. The institutions that are rich of heart and pride themselves on traditions and rules that are in no way essential for their sanctification or their apostolate will not be able to make a new start. They will be like the rich young man: he could not detach his heart from his wealth, and could not take up the risk of following Christ into the unknown. He preferred the security of his possessions to the insecurity of the Spirit. He missed the divine opportunity offered to him, and we do not even know his name today.

God offers an opportunity to every institute now: each should hold an examination of conscience and ask if it is so poor in spirit that it can receive a new inspiration and follow it out. There should be no illusion: this is a question of life or death for every religious body. It is liberating for us all to state the problem clearly. There are times when charity and courtesy require that our speech should be circumspect and difficulties avoided; there are other times when the same charity and respect for each other necessitates clear statements and examination of the consequences of action.

It is truth and courage that will free us from all our bonds, make us poor of heart and receptive to the graces the Holy Spirit wants to give in abundance today.

4

Journey in Faith: Obedience

Perhaps it is well to say in the beginning that, even if we are not able to explain fully the mystery of religious obedience (because it does remain a mystery), we are certainly able to live the mystery of obedience. This is true not only of obedience but of many other Christian virtues. We cannot explain fully what Christian faith is, what Christian hope is, and what Christian charity is. But, with the help of the Holy Spirit, a child of God can have the divine strength that comes from hope and charity.

Living the virtue of obedience should not, therefore, be confused with the explanation of the virtue of obedience. A religious may be perfectly able to live up to the highest ideals of the virtue of obedience without being able to explain it; and, perhaps, a theologian who can explain the virtue of obedience will not live up to its highest ideals.

THE OBEDIENCE OF CHRIST

To explain what Christian religious obedience means, the Council refers to Paul's Letter to the Philippians (2, 5-8), which reads in the Jerusalem Bible version:

In your minds you must be the same as Christ Jesus: His state was divine, yet he did not cling to his equality with God but emptied himself to assume the condition of a slave, and became as men are; and being as all men are, he was humbler yet, even to accepting death, death on a cross (Phil 2, 5–8).

Two modern translations read:

Have this mind among yourselves, which you have in Christ Jesus, who, though he was in the form of God, did not count equality with God a thing to be grasped, but emptied himself, taking the form of a servant, being born in the likeness of men. And being found in human form he humbled himself and became obedient unto death, even death upon a cross (*Revised Standard Version*).

Let Christ Jesus be your example as to what your attitude should be. For he, who had always been God by nature, did not cling to his prerogatives as God's equal, but stripped himself of all privilege by consenting to be a slave by nature and being born as mortal man. And, having become man, he humbled himself by living a life of utter obedience, even to the extent of dying, *and the death he died was the death of a common criminal* (J. B. Phillips, *The New Testament in Modern English*).

Some commentary may serve to give a clearer conception of what the obedience of Christ was and what our obedience must be. It must be the same as Christ's. The obedience of the members of a body cannot be different from the obedience of the head. The obedience of Christ is the key to the obedience of a Christian and, all the more, of a religious: "In your minds you must be the same as Christ Jesus." This means that we all should have a practical attitude of mind and a practical disposition of heart that correspond to the attitude and disposition of the mind and heart of Christ, or better, that is *identical* with the attitude and the disposition of Christ. We are members of his mystical body, and he is the head. The disposition of the head should be diffused in the whole body. Thus an identity should be achieved between the mind of Christ and the mind of a Christian, between the heart of Christ and the heart of a Christian. We have to put these Pauline expressions into the context of his whole doctrine on the mystical body, all Christians being members of the body, of which the head is Christ. In this way, we shall understand Christian obedience as a reflection or diffusion of the attitude of Christ in the whole body. In this way, our obedience will be identical with the obedience of Christ.

What exactly was the obedience of Christ? Paul's answer begins in verse 6: "His form was divine, yet he did not cling to his equality with God."

In other words: although he, Christ, was subsisting in the form of divinity, in the form of God (that is, he was God), he did not consider divinity as a prize to be coveted, he did not reach out covetously for divine glory. St. Paul's first statement is that Christ was God from the beginning. Then he explains the modality of Christ's incarnation. When he took on our human nature, it would have been perfectly natural for him to be in a state of glory (as he was after his resurrection), but this is precisely what he did not covet in his mortal body. He was true God and true man, and since he was true God, he had a right to be in the glory of God always, even in his mortal human nature.

But he did not covet this glory; he preferred to take the form of a slave: He "emptied himself, to assume the conditions of a slave, and became as men are," that is, he wanted to be in the same condition in which we all are, in the condition of a mortal man without any visible and tangible sign of glory. He much preferred to be one who serves, that is, to submit himself to ordinary human conditions. He submitted himself to his Father through the intermediaries of this created world—persons, events, and various institutions, legal and liturgical, and in many other ways. This is what St. Paul calls the "emptying" of Christ; "He emptied himself" of a glory that was due him. He did not want glory but rather, for our sake, he wanted a lowly condition, a simple condition. He wanted to be a humble man, subject to the limitations and sufferings that we have to go through. In this lowly condition, he preferred to submit himself to his Father and to created things and persons that showed him the will of his Father.

This submission to God through creatures who manifest God's will to us will be the key to obedience, to any obedience, and in particular to religious obedience. An obedient person submits himself to God and, because of his lowly condition, he submits himself to created persons and created things through whom, or through which, the will of God is being made manifest to him. This thought is the precise key that opens up the mystery of obedience.

Verse 8 confirms and concludes the explanation of Christ's humility: "And being as all men are, he was humbler yet, even to accepting death, death on a cross." Humility and obedience are used in a very similar sense. Obedience, for Christ, meant to accept his Father's plan, to accept his Father's will, through many different channels: through diverse persons, through various events, through human institutions. Christ manifested his love for his Father by submitting himself to these intermediaries, messengers of his Father's will.

Christ himself did not have any superior on earth or in heaven; he was equal with his Father. His obedience consisted in submitting himself in his human nature to the will of his Father. His Father's will was manifested to him internally through the Spirit, externally through this created universe. Although, externally, he subjected himself to created intermediaries, internally he maintained a personal contact with his Father, and he remained a free person. When he submitted himself to any created event, or any created person, he did so out of respect for his Father. He practiced obedience, but at the same time he remained perfectly free because his obedience was a subjection to his Father and not to any human person or to any other creature or event in this universe.

The Fathers of the Church like to point out that Christ, through his obedience, restored what we lost in Adam. The great sin of the first man was that he wanted to be like God. The serpent, the tempter, promised him that he would be like God, he would know good and evil. In fact, we are told by scholars that the original text does not say, or does not mean, that he will *know* good and evil, but that he will *decide* what is good and evil. It belongs to the divine power to make a supreme decision, to say what is good and what is evil; this belongs to God, to no one else. This is precisely what the tempter promised to the first man: if you assert your freedom, if you reject God, you will be like him, you will *decide* what is good and evil, you will not have to abide by his commands: you become the supreme law to yourself.

The first Adam coveted a divine power, and fell through his disobedience; and through his sin we all have been wounded. The second Adam, Christ, in his mortal body, did not covet equality with God, but became obedient and, through his obedience, we all have been healed. His emptiness made us rich.

THE OBEDIENCE OF A CHRISTIAN

To grasp the meaning of Christian obedience it is necessary to draw a parallel between the obedience of Christ and the obedience of a Christian, remaining within the context of St. Paul's thought. The obedience of a religious is not different from the obedience of a Christian, although it may be more exacting, going somehow deeper in its intensity.

The basis of Christian obedience is this identity of mind and heart with Christ. He is the head of the body and we are the members, and the members cannot have a different life from the head. The obedience and humility of the head ought to be fully, and without any compromise, in the members as well. Therefore, the obedience of Christ will be our obedience. It is not enough to say that the obedience of Christ should be a model of our obedience. Although this statement is true, it is not the whole truth. A model remains always something external, but our share in the obedience of Christ is internal. There is a living and internal connection with Christ, between the head and the members, between Christ and his Christians, a sharing of Christ's virtue within his mystical body. In obedience, as in other virtues, there is a unity within the body, a unity between the head and the members. This unity is real because we are incorporated into the body of Christ, and we are led by his Spirit to obey the Father.

In fact, the Council uses this expression: "Under the influence of the Holy Spirit, religious submit themselves to their superiors" (Abbott, *op. cit.*, p. 476). In the matter of obedience, too, we live in the Spirit of Christ: the same eternal Spirit who lives in Christ lives in us, and he, the

Spirit, moves the whole mystical body, the head and the members, to obey the Father. So that when we say that we should have the same mind that Christ has, we mean a deep and real unity with Christ; not with him merely as an external example, but with him in a communion in grace, a participation of his grace. It could not be anything less.

Now, we are adopted children of God, and we therefore have the glory of the children of God: this divine glory is in us. St. Paul says:

> I think that what we suffer in this life can never be compared to the glory, as yet unrevealed, which is waiting for us. The whole creation is eagerly waiting for God to reveal his sons. It was not for any fault on the part of creation that it was made unable to attain its purpose, it was made so by God; but creation still retains the hope of being freed, like us, from its slavery to decadence, to enjoy the same freedom and glory as the children of God. From the beginning till now the entire creation, as we know, has been groaning in one great act of giving birth; and not only creation, but all of us who possess the first-fruits of the Spirit, we too groan inwardly as we wait for our bodies to be set free (Rom 8, 18–21).

That is the glory of the children of God; something of the glory of the Risen Christ is present in us all; we already share his eternal glory. But, at the same time, Christ in his goodness makes us share also his condition of emptiness, his condition of humility. His glory is in us internally, but is not manifest externally. Some persons who have a great and intense gift of faith are able to look through a human person in such a way that they do not see the human accidentals. They go immediately to the essentials and find the glory of the children of God in the other person; they are able to respect and love a child of God independently of

any external appearance. A few Christians reach such perfection in this life, but most of us can hope to reach it in
heaven only.

Because we are children of God, we are not subject to
any human person or to any creature. The children of God
cannot be subject to anybody else but God himself. This is
important to grasp. Unless we know about this absolute
freedom and independence of the child of God, we shall
not be able to understand his subjection. We possess something of the glory of the divine nature and therefore we
are fully independent; we are subject only to the divine
Persons, but if God passes on his authority to a human
person, then we have to obey God by obeying that human
person. Even then, a child of God will fully retain his
independence and freedom; but he will use his freedom to
submit himself to God. It is clear that he will not be able
to do so, unless he has a vision of faith that God is coming
to him through human persons; unless he has a strong
faith that these persons will lead him to God; and finally,
unless he has such a great love that he is able to overcome
the repugnance of his humanity to accept God's presence
in the words of a human person. And it is in this sense that
we have to empty ourselves, to renounce any manifestation
of the glory of the children of God that is in us, and accept
the humble state in which we are subject to God's will as it
comes to us through created persons—and in a more general way, through the whole of this created universe.

Christ's obedience embraced everything: he obeyed
his Father in personal commands he received from those
who appeared to have authority over him; he obeyed his
Father as his will became manifest by laws, institutions,
and ordinary events. We, too, have to obey God's will as it
is manifested to us through persons in authority, through

laws, institutions, and ordinary events. This obedience rests on a vision of faith that enables us to see that somehow the whole universe is divine, bringing us the message of God.

A brief remark about the spirituality of St. Ignatius Loyola may be in order. The great innovation of Ignatius in religious life was that he pushed the limits of the cloister to the ends of the world. He did not want to abandon the cloister; he did not want to give up liturgy; but he widened the limits of the cloister and included all activities in the service of God within a divine liturgy. This is, for all practical purposes, the essence of Jesuit spirituality. It is contemplative, it is active, it is cloistered (if you like), provided the limits of the cloister extend as far as men can go. It is liturgical, provided that all human activity which springs from a desire to serve God, is conceived as belonging to the worship of God. That is why contemplation and action cannot really be distinguished in St. Ignatius' spirituality; whatever one does, one is moving about in God, one's prayer or action is a response to a divine invitation.

There is no situation in human life in which a Christian answer is not possible. It may well be that the Christian answer is, "My Father, if it is possible, let this cup pass me by" (Mt 26, 39)—to suffer, not to rebel. Even to be impatient because of human frailty but *not fully*—even that is still Christian. There is a possibility of a liturgical answer in this sense to everything; an answer inspired or supported by the Holy Spirit.

The Christian takes the form of a servant, renouncing the manifestation of his glory here on earth, which is due to him as a child of God. He takes the form of a slave, of a lowly person who is subject to God and does the will of God as that will becomes manifest to him in ordinary

events, in ordinary persons, and in ordinary human institutions. In this way, he becomes obedient to God as St.
Paul says: "even unto accepting death, death on a cross."

There is, consequently, a genuine parallel, even more,
an identity, between the obedience of Christ and the obedience of a Christian. Whatever discussions have arisen in
the Church today about the concept and the practice of
obedience, they cannot touch the substance of Christian
obedience, because it is the obedience of Christ. His obedience will not and cannot change: it will remain the same
forever. Christian obedience is an obedience to the point
of emptying oneself, in accepting the will of God as it
becomes manifest through created channels, unto death,
unto whatever death God may give to a Christian. If there
are any discussions, they concern the modalities of obedience, the practical way of fulfilling this duty to obey and, if
there is any new vision in the Church, it regards again the
practical way of fulfilling this duty of obedience and not in
destroying the traditional concept of full obedience, which
is a full sacrifice.

OBEDIENCE ROOTED IN FAITH, HOPE, AND CHARITY

Obedience is rooted in the three theological virtues, faith,
hope, and charity. In their context alone the virtue of
obedience takes on its full meaning, and receives that balanced interpretation which is so necessary.

The Council states that religious obedience is based
on faith. One could add, in particular, that faith in the
divine quality of this created world is especially required
for the virtue of obedience. I cannot "empty" myself and
obey God, unless I believe that persons living in this
world, the events happening in it, and things existing in it

are the channels of the will of God for me. Without this faith in the divine quality of the world, without understanding that this world is the incarnation of a plan that was conceived in the mind and heart of God, without this faith and without this vision, no one can really obey. Unless I believe that persons, events, and created things are able to be, and *are,* channels of the will of God for me, I will not, I cannot obey the will of God that should be manifest to me through them. Frequently, when we fail in obedience, we fail because we do not have this vision and this understanding of the divine quality of the world.

It is easier to understand now the deep connection in the mind of St. Ignatius between the two fundamental virtues that the members of his Society were expected to possess: obedience and faith that finds God in all things; they go together. You cannot make obedience the basic rule of your life, unless you believe that this universe is revealing to you the mind and the heart of God. This faith could be called also a biblical vision of the world, or even more: Christ's vision of the world. For Christ, his coming into this world was a coming into his Father's house. To Christ, everything spoke about the mind and the will of his Father; the created world, for him, was the image of his Father. A Christian should be of the same mind: he should believe that created persons, created things, and ordinary events lead him to God; that is, they are instruments of the grace of God for him, they bring him new happiness, they lead him to God. The virtue of faith is the foundation of the virtue of obedience.

The divine virtue of trust, of hope, centers on God's fidelity. I hope that he will save me, and that he will give me all the means necessary to attain my eternal happiness. Those means may be supernatural and natural. Since they can be natural means, the divine virtue of hope may have for its object earthly things as well. Faith is entirely centered on God; but hope can be centered on a person or a created object as well. Accordingly, through the virtue of hope and trust, I give myself to God because I know with certainty that the will of God, as it becomes manifest to me through created things, will lead me to God, and I hope that, through them, God will give me full happiness. Without this hope, I could not obey. The virtue of hope belongs to the soul of obedience.

This virtue of hope includes trust in God's providence. To understand this, we have to consider again that we are members of the mystical body of Christ. Now, God the Father takes care of the whole body: head and members—Christ and his brothers. His providence is the same for both head and members. He, the Father, has the same solicitous care for us that he had for Jesus, his Son. It is difficult for us to accept this, to believe really and effectively in our dignity and the generous love of God. Yet, the providence of God for us is no less than it was for Christ because the Father looks after the whole body of Christ with the same love and care that he lavished on the head. To believe in this truth, and to hope in this loving care of God are essential for one striving fully to practice the virtue of obedience.

Finally, obedience should be understood and practiced in the context of divine love, divine charity. This love and charity mean that I want to give myself and all I have to God, without expecting any reward; I want to enrich the person I love. Obedience will frequently demand this giving through creatures, through intermediaries. I offer myself to God, I want to give all that I have to God, but, through obedience, I have to expend myself on human creatures and on building the kingdom of God by doing very ordinary work in this world. I would love to meet God, and be with him, but he orders me to remain— in the classroom, among noisy children. This means a sacrifice for a child of God. In fact, this giving in love, giving all that I have to God, cannot be done without sacrifice.

Sacrifice is frequently conceived of as an act by which I destroy something. I give up something and, because I give it up, or do not use it, I say I sacrifice it. This is obviously not the full explanation of a sacrifice. It is an accidental aspect. The real and full meaning of the word sacrifice is an act by which I achieve a greater union with God. If I sacrifice all my worldly goods for God's sake, the main point is not in leaving all the worldly goods, but in freeing myself in order to achieve a greater union with God. What really matters is this positive aspect, but the negative side is bound to be nearly always present. Since my nature is human, since I feel the weight of my own sins, of my own evil inclinations, every step towards a deeper union with the invisible God may be resented by my fallen nature. Moreover, the transformation of simple human nature into a sharing of the divine nature, (as is our vocation) may sometimes imply the destroying of some values, good in themselves, but which, in these particular circumstances, are an impediment towards a full union with God. The main point in sacrifice is not in destroying something, but in trying to achieve a fuller union with God. In order to achieve this fuller union, I discard created things, I free myself from impediments; and this freeing hurts my human nature and I call it a sacrifice, but the real meaning of sacrifice does not lie there. It lies in *union*.

To obey God means precisely to achieve a greater

union with God. It means a greater intensity of love, giving more and more. This giving may incidentally hurt my humanity because it is not yet fully adapted to the purity of love. This is just part of my progress towards God: the pilgrim's progress.

Obedience, then, can be called sacrifice in two different senses. First, it is sacrifice in a positive sense; it means a greater union with God in love. My will is sacrificed: it is united with God's will. Second, obedience is sacrifice in a negative sense; it means suffering in my human nature. This suffering follows from the weakness and impurity of my human nature, which is hurt by the great and spiritual love that is expressed in an act of obedience.

The full meaning of obedience lies in this loving union with God: I give myself and the best I have, my will, to him. A deep union is achieved; my offering is a spiritual sacrifice. We see now that obedience cannot exist without faith, hope, and charity; it is a particular manifestation of the three theological virtues.

RELIGIOUS OBEDIENCE

Let us begin by saying that religious obedience is an attitude or a virtue of a whole community which forms a unity in the mystical body of Christ. Christ obeyed his Father; in the same way, the whole Church has to obey God and a whole religious order has to obey the Church.

It follows that obedience in a religious community should not be conceived of exclusively in an individualistic way, as the virtue of the individual persons. It is certainly that, as we shall see, but above all it is the virtue of the whole community, which, head and members, has to obey together as one body, and subject itself to the will of God.

The head of a religious community and the members form a unity, and they all have to submit themselves to God and enable God to realize his plan in this world. Obedience, therefore, is a social virtue. We have to insist on this unity of a community, because superiors and subjects are not separate entities; they form one body, and this body is called to do the will of God. Therefore, the search for the will of God should go on in the whole community. The whole community has the mission and the means to find the will of God, although the part that the superior plays in finding the will of God, and the part that the members of the community play, will be different ones, as head and members are different in a body.

Only by keeping in mind that obedience is a social virtue shall we understand the complexity of personal obedience. Every member of a community will have to search for the will of God, for his will as regards this particular community; and with humility and discretion, every member must inspire the superiors. Finally, the superior will have to make decisions, and this act will be his, not that of the members. But even in making a decision, the superior will make it in an attitude of humility: "I make this decision because I conceive it to be the will of God for us"; not with an attitude of superiority: "I want to impose my will." The fundamental attitude of a superior should be obedience: he should be of the same mind as Christ Jesus who was obedient. Christ's disposition in his heart was not to command, but to obey, to be a servant. Equally, the fundamental attitude of the subject should be to obey, taking his own place in the social body, in the community. Therefore, if the superior makes a decision, he should make it in obedience to the will of God; because God wants him to make that decision. If the subject has to carry out an order, he should do so in union with Christ who is obedient to his Father. The virtue of obedience should penetrate the whole social body.

But, to repeat, the practice of obedience will be different in the head and in the members. There will be in the community a *communion* in Christ's obedience; all will be sharing in different ways the obedience of Christ. A small cell in the great body of Christ will submit itself to the will of God: this is religious obedience in a community.

The search for the will of God can be painful for us; it was never painful for Christ himself: he had a clear vision of his Father's will. During the first years of his public ministry, every time his enemies wanted to arrest him, he hid himself, he avoided them, because he had a clear vision that it was not the will of his Father that he should as yet be arrested, that he should suffer. When the hour of his Father came, he went to meet the man who betrayed him, and all those who came to take him, because he had the clear vision that "his hour" had come. Christ had an infallible vision to know to what event, through what persons, through what created things, the will of his Father was being made manifest to him.

We do not have this vision. We have to use our human intelligence, our human instincts; we have to use our vision of faith (much more limited than the vision of Christ), and we have to institute a search to find God's will. This search should be in proportion to the case concerned; it should not be overdone. Yet, to search for the will of God will frequently mean a real effort, a genuine exertion of our natural and supernatural capacities.

It is clear, therefore, why a superior has to take advice from all sides, and why a subject has the duty, the sacred office, to inspire the superior: to find God's will for his greater glory is the duty of the whole community. When this process of finding the will of God has been concluded, according to the importance of the case, God's will is that the superior should make a decision. It may not be the most perfect one, it may be just a reasonably good one, according to the light that God gives, then and there.

The community should be united in trying to find God's will, but the search should be concluded by the superior's decision. In this way, the will of God will be found and established in a community. Anybody who would exclude this painstaking process of finding the will of God would be unduly divinizing either the person of the superior or of the subject. We have to find the will of God according to our condition, using our human intelligence, strengthened by the help that comes from faith, hope, and charity. Our vision will always be dimmed by a certain obscurity that will necessitate a painful search. Our Christian life will always be marked by a certain stability and steadiness, but those gifts of the Spirit will always be coupled with a painstaking search, efforts, and tensions. This is true of the individual Christian; it is true also of a Christian community trying to be obedient to God's will.

RELIGIOUS OBEDIENCE IS A PERSONAL COVENANT WITH GOD

Obedience should also be a personal virtue in every Christian, in every religious. We all should have the same mind that Christ had, and the mind of Christ can be gathered from the Scriptures.

He came to do his Father's will:

> and this is what he said, on coming into the world: You who wanted no sacrifice or oblation, prepared a body for

me. You took no pleasure in holocausts or sacrifices for sin; then I said, just as I was commanded in the scroll of the book, 'God, here I am! I am coming to obey your will' (Heb 10, 5–7).

Christ's whole life was a life of obedience: "because I have come from heaven, not to do my own will, but to do the will of the one who sent me" (Jn 6, 38).

He accepted the Cross in a spirit of obedience, and prayed: " 'My Father,' he said, 'if it is possible, let this cup pass me by. Nevertheless, let it be as you, not I, would have it' " (Mt 26, 39).

Through his obedience we are saved:

> During his life on earth, he offered up prayer and entreaty, aloud and in silent tears, to the one who had the power to save him out of death, and he submitted so humbly that his prayer was heard. Although he was Son, he learnt to obey through suffering; but having been made perfect, he became for all who obey him the source of eternal salvation and was acclaimed by God with the title of high priest of the order of Melchizedek (Heb 5, 7–10).

To follow Christ means to have the same mind that he had, and to have the same determination to do the will of his Father. This determination to do the will of the Father is the basic condition for personal obedience. One can make mistakes in the modalities; one can have more or less initiative then one should. All that is perfectly possible; not only possible, but it is bound to happen with any good religious at one time or another. What should not be lacking is the determination, the readiness to do the will of God.

When one tries to be active and responsible, one does so because one wants to obey God. However, one does not want to be independent of the will of God, seeking an emancipation from his power, as the first man did who wanted to be like God and to decide what is good and what is evil.

There could be some confusion on this point. Some persons, perhaps unwittingly, through lack of reflection, may conceive active and responsible obedience as an emancipation from the will of God. It is not and it should not be. To be active and to be responsible is the right way of conforming myself to the will of God.

Because among human persons the finding of the will of God can be a complex process, we have to search for that will; since we do not have the clear vision that Christ had, the Church comes to our help if we consecrate ourselves to the practice of obedience in a religious institute. The Church provides the institute with a whole scale of means to find the will of God. There will be a series of superiors. Frequently there is a delicate interplay, as when a case is brought from one superior to another, precisely in order to establish the will of God with greater certainty. Superiors and subjects have to take part in this process (sometimes painful) to find his will.

If anybody asked what is the difference between the obedience of a Christian in general and the obedience of a religious, the answer would be that in substance they are the same. Both a lay Christian and a religious share the obedience of Christ when they obey *in* him, *through* him, and *with* him their Father in heaven. However, the obedience of a consecrated religious has its particular aspects: it covers a broader field; it is more intense; it takes place in a well determined community, part of the mystical body; it is sealed by a vow, which is a consecration. Through the vow of obedience, through the consecration that represents the vow of a religious, a personal covenant is established between God and the religious, similar to that which existed between God and Abraham who obeyed the divine call.

Here, perhaps, it is necessary to say something about religious vows and consecration. We conceive of our vows as an offering to God, as giving something to God. This, in a way, is true; but again, it is not the whole truth and it is not even the better part of the truth. The better part of the truth is that God gives something to us. The gift we receive from him takes an external expression in the pronouncing of the vow. We understand the nature of religious vows better if we consider the liturgy of the consecration of a priest rather than if we consider the usual ceremony of religious vows.

The consecration of a priest, which is a sacrament, shows fully that the person receiving the consecration receives a personal gift from God. He has been chosen for an office by the mysterious providence of God. He did not choose his vocation; God chose him. Therefore, the liturgy of the consecration is centered on this gift of God. God is giving something to the person. In the early Church, a similar type of liturgy existed for the consecration of a virgin, although it was never considered a sacrament. The ceremonies expressed the truth that it was not so much the young woman who gave herself to God but it was God who consecrated her to his service through the bishop who, in the name of the Church, imposed the veil on a virgin. Since the virgin accepted God's gift, she was consecrated to God and belonged to God: she became a sacred person.

To take religious vows is to accept a sacred gift from God. Unfortunately, in our present conception the emphasis has shifted from the grace received to the formal pronouncing of the vows, to such an extent that sometimes it is to be feared that those taking the vows do not fully realize that it is God who is consecrating them, through an act of the Church; they think the principal aspect is that they give something to God. This shift of emphasis is sometimes expressed in the very ceremony. The old consecration of virgins was a joyful ceremony, one akin to any ceremony that is fitting to the Paschal season. The Spirit of God is being diffused in the heart of man, and it is diffused in a particular way as a particular gift into the heart of this particular person. The Church seals it by a liturgical action; therefore the person belongs to God.

Now, what is the virtue of religious obedience? A personal call from God to a human person, calling him to give himself to God, to the service of God in a closer way; and, in particular, to do the will of God as God manifests it to him in the Church, through his superiors. Could one say that it is a call to be incorporated even more deeply into the Church?

The fuller meaning of the religious vows lies in the fact that such vows are the fruit and the expression of a gratuitous and free call from God. They are internal graces given to a person, whom God calls to serve the Church in a particular way, in a community within the Church, by making the vows of chastity, poverty, and obedience; or better, by *receiving* this threefold gift from God.

Now, any call from God to a human person to obey God in a particular way includes a promise from God that he will lead that person. He will lead through human superiors to a great spiritual perfection; we do not know exactly how great, how intense, but great according to the plan of God. And thus the person who receives this call, who receives this promise and accepts it, concludes a personal covenant with God. God promises through his Spirit to take care of him and, externally, the Church guarantees the promise.

Since this call will lead towards a transformation into God through intermediaries and created channels, it will include necessarily some sacrifice in the sense of suffering. It cannot be in any other way, because this transformation of our fallen human nature to the image of Christ is a process painful for our humanity. Therefore, to follow this path of obedience, to follow the personal call of God, will mean to share somehow the sacrifice of Christ on the cross. No one can escape this sacrifice. In one form or another it will come for all of us. But the sacrifice will always be followed by a particular blessing on the part of God; he promises that an obedient person will be enriched and, through him, many others will be enriched. Christ's obedience was the source of our redemption:

> But God raised him high and gave him the name which is above all other names so that all beings in the heavens, on earth and in the underworld, should bend the knee at the name of Jesus and that every tongue should acclaim Jesus Christ as Lord, to the glory of God the Father (Phil 2, 9–11).

We can say that the pattern of any religious vocation is the pattern of the call of Abraham. In his case, there was a free call from God; God chose Abraham in order to achieve a closer union with him. Then, God consecrated Abraham to himself through a particular promise he made when he appeared to Abraham in the form of a living flame. And God was with Abraham in his long wanderings. He did not save him from sorrows and suffering, but blessed him with a son, and made him the father of all believers.

Just as God took care of Abraham, whom he called, so will he take care of religious. In the Church, within a community, within the context of rules and constitutions and regulations, God will lead the religious towards a closer union with himself. The religious who follows God's call will normally experience a great deal of suffering: so did Abraham. A good religious will make many mistakes in the process; but he will finally find a closer union with God, a closer union, not in the sense that we find it in rather popular spiritual books. In all probability, few of the real saints are recognized by the Church; most of them remain hidden behind imperfections and mistakes. They will be revealed in the other world, and it is good for us that it should be so.

To vow obedience to God, as a member of a religious institute, is to accept a personal gift from God, to conclude a covenant with God—through the Church. This personal covenant is our strength. Each religious person who is consecrated to God somehow shares in the grace of Abraham. The religious, too, is called to serve God in a particular way and by accepting God's call and believing in his promise, he takes up a new and personal vocation. He will serve God by obeying him in human superiors, within the context of the constitutions and the rules of a religious institute and with a particularly deep incorporation into the visible Church.

It remains now to comment on the text of the Decree with a view to connecting the theological ideas with the text.

SOME COMMENTS ON THE TEXT

In the Decree on Religious (*Perfectae Caritatis*), the Council's doctrine on obedience is summed up in paragraph 14 (Abbott, *op. cit.*, p. 476).

"Through the profession of obedience, religious offer to God a total dedication of their own wills as a sacrifice of themselves." The term sacrifice is to be taken in the context of God's gift and God's covenant. God offers me a personal gift: to lead me in the hierarchical Church, through human superiors, towards perfection. By taking my vow, I accept God's offer, and through the Church, God seals the covenant. God wants me to serve him with fidelity. This service necessarily includes the dedication of my own will. No one can dedicate his will to another without making a sacrifice. It will be a sacrifice in the sense of leaving behind his own human will, but still more in the sense of achieving a fuller union with God.

"[By this sacrifice religious] unite themselves with greater steadiness and security to the saving will of God." It is not uncommon to hear that by taking the vow of obedience the religious saves himself from any preoccupation. This is true to some extent only; because active and responsible obedience will give the religious plenty of preoccupation. Religious obedience does not mean passivity, but the entering in a deeper way into the active life of the Holy Spirit. At the same time, it is true that the practice of obedience will give the religious peace and relaxation. God promised to be with him and to lead him, through the decisions of superiors. Sometimes it may be a difficult question for a religious to go, or not to go, to higher superiors; but, finally, he knows that there will be a point where he will have to stop, and the will of God will be manifest for him. He is more firmly and stably united to the saving will of God; that is, obedience will lead him to spiritual union with God. This is what God promises.

God does not necessarily promise that, through obedience, he will keep a particular institute going. Unless the institute corresponds to all the graces that God offers, even the obedience of the best of its members will not save it.

"In this way [religious] follow the pattern of Jesus Christ, who came to do the Father's will." The texts cited in the Decree are:

> But Jesus said: 'My food is to do the will of the one who sent me, and to complete his work' (Jn 4, 34).
>
> 'I can only judge as I am told to judge, and my judging is just, because my aim is to do not my own will, but the will of him who sent me' (Jn 5, 30).
>
> Then I said, just as I was commanded in the scroll of the book, 'God, here I am! I am coming to obey your will' (Heb 10, 7).

"Under the influence of the Holy Spirit, religious submit themselves to their superiors, whom faith presents as God's representatives, and through whom they are guided to the service of all their brothers in Christ." The obedient religious is moved by the Holy Spirit. The Council draws our attention to the fact that religious obedience is not a military obedience. By its very essence, there cannot be any act of obedience that does not proceed from the Holy Spirit. The inspiration of the Spirit, his prompting, is the soul of obedience. But this soul has to take on flesh; therefore, the motion of the Holy Spirit will be in harmony with the external order or command that comes to me from the superior in the name of God.

Perfect obedience includes a certain gentleness, readiness, and facility that comes from the Holy Spirit. At the same time, it includes a fidelity to the external command, to the external rules, to the external laws. Any comparison with strictly military obedience and drill would be a distortion of religious obedience, for military obedience, as it is understood in the ordinary sense, is more external than internal.

In what sense should the subject consider the superior as representing God? To have the right idea will help us to practice the right type of obedience. Clearly, the subject should never consider the superior a sort of divine person. Moreover, the subject should never consider the superior (unless the superior is the pope, a bishop, in some cases a priest) as having a particular charism attached to his office by divine right, although, obviously enough, a superior may be a charismatic person. To exaggerate these points, even while meaning well, would be very dangerous for the spirit of obedience; for, sooner or later, the subject will be disappointed. One day, he will discover that the superior is a human being who does not have this particular charism by divine right. He, the subject, should humbly accept God's real world. He should consider the superior as a human person through whom God is manifesting his will. With the help of the Holy Spirit, the subject should recognize the manifestation of the will of God in the words and wishes of the superior, and, at the same time, recognize the human framework.

This distinction is vital, because it will save the subject from a servile obedience and will make him obedient to God. What is servile obedience? It is an obedience to the human person *only:* the subject wants to please the man, he is not much interested in God. He wants the human favor of a poor human person. Therefore, when his opinion is asked, he instinctively, perhaps subconsciously, will tell the superior what he knows the superior likes to hear. Such behavior is not the sharing of Christ's pure and refreshing obedience to his Father.

An obedient person, who is in possession of the supernatural virtue of obedience, will recognize the message of God when it comes through the superior, and will subject himself to that message fully, whatever it may be. He will never deny that God may personally assist the superior. At the same time, retaining his freedom as a child of God, he will serve God and not a man.

Precisely because the manifestation of God's will comes through a human person who is not infallible, a certain amount of healthy and religious free play, in the way of exchanges of information, dialog, appeals, is necessary between the subject and the superior in order to find the will of God. But this "free play" concerns the modality, not the substance of obedience. It is a concerted effort to find out God's will, and not a means to emancipate oneself from obedience. Finally, it is the superior who should make the decision, and then the subject is bound to obey, unless he knows clearly, in his conscience, that the order is sinful.

The divine guarantee of leading the subject to a union with God is authentic even if the superior's command, in the circumstances, is mistaken. The divine guarantee would not apply only if the superior ordered something sinful, and the subject, realizing this, nevertheless obeyed. Fortunately, this is not a practical problem. Servile obedience is a practical problem and every superior ought to be very much on his guard to discourage servility and to encourage the divine freedom of the children of God.

The free obedience of the children of God should be

encouraged by every means. Blessed is the superior who can do that; it means that he has arrived at a very high degree of unselfishness. It will do untold good to an institution if it is known among the members that nobody is particularly favored just because he happens to think in the same way as the superior, provided all are genuinely ready to obey. A healthy spirit will reign within the community. But if it is known that no inspiration is ever tolerated and listened to other than that of the superior, the good health of the community will be in danger. How can the Holy Spirit, in such circumstances, help the institute by inspiring the members? That is why, on the whole, external signs of reverence should be moderate. In a balanced form they should be retained, because they are the expression of the faith of the subject that God is working through the superior. The practice of a long-founded religious order provides a good example of such balance. This order certainly retains external signs of reverence towards the superior: everywhere, he takes the first place, in the church, in the refectory. But, in the refectory, the last in rank is served first and the superior last. Here is a fine balance between respecting Christ in the superior and feeding Christ in the subject. Not every institute would wish to imitate this practice, but each institute should pray for the wisdom which is expressed in it.

"Thus did Christ Himself out of submission to his Father minister to the brethren and surrender His life as a ransom for many." The texts quoted are:

> . . . just as the Son of Man came not to be served but to serve, and to give his life as a ransom for many (Mt 20, 28).
>
> I am the good shepherd; I know my own and my own know me, just as the Father knows me and I know the

Father; and I lay down my life for my sheep. And there are other sheep I have that are not of this fold, and these I have to lead as well. They too will listen to my voice, and there will be only one flock, and one shepherd. The Father loves me, because I lay down my life in order to take it up again. No one takes it from me; I lay it down of my own free will, and as it is in my power to lay it down, so it is in my power to take it up again; and this is the command I have been given by my Father (Jn 10, 14–18).

In this way we are all to come to unity in our faith and in our knowledge of the Son of God, until we become the perfect Man, fully mature with the fulness of Christ himself (Eph 4, 13).

The virtue of obedience, as the Council conceives it, is essentially a virtue in the service of the Church. By practicing obedience, we are building the Church. We are building a particular community, and, through it, we are making the whole Church stronger and working for the expansion of the kingdom of God. That is, obedience should never be considered as a means to individual perfection only; it should also be conceived of as one of the best instruments for the expansion of the kingdom of God. By obedience, we insert ourselves into the life of the Church more closely. By our consecration to obedience, we insert ourselves more closely into the visible structure of the Church and through our practice of obedience into the invisible structure of the Church. No one can say exactly how, because we are touching here the mystery of God; but precisely because we are better inserted into the life of the Church, there is a freer circulation of graces through us. We make the whole Church stronger internally and externally, and we are able to build the Church in a more intense way. Religious obedience is the virtue of the apostles.

> Realizing that they are giving service to the upbuilding of Christ's body according to God's design, let them bring to the execution of commands and to the discharge of assignments entrusted to them the resources of their minds and wills, and their gifts of nature and grace. Lived in this manner, religious obedience will not diminish the dignity of the human person but will rather lead it to maturity in consequence of that enlarged freedom which belongs to the sons of God (Abbott, *ibid.*).

The Council seems to state a paradox: subjection will lead to maturity and obedience to enlarged freedom. How can there be harmony between such opposite attitudes and qualities? How can the paradox be explained in meaningful terms; how can maturity and freedom be experienced in subjection and obedience?

The answer is to be found in the purification of our concept of obedience. Internal Christian obedience to God has to be distinguished from its external manifestation in a religious institute. The former is absolute: I am subject to God in all. The latter is relative: I have to obey a man so far as God's authority is with him. To be subject to God means to depend on God as the source of life and existence. To obey him is nothing else than to receive his abundance. Obedience is a poor way of expressing a union between God and his creature. To be subject to a religious superior means to honor in him God's authority as far as he received it. Wisdom in obedience will consist in knowing how far the authority of God in man extends. To obey more than this divine authority would warrant is to destroy the dignity of a child of God, to obey less is to refuse to be in touch with the living source of life through cre-

ated persons. To help us to discover the fine balance necessary for the practice of religious obedience, the Council
gives some indication of its real nature. It is for the up-
building of Christ's body. In negative terms, it is not for
establishing a perfect order of the day, or a neat uniformity in the community; it is for a far more important purpose: the building of the kingdom. It is through obedience
that a person is inserted into the design that God has for
the life and the work of his visible Church. This is the
dignity of obedience: its scope is as broad as that of the
mystical Christ. But when this obedience is confused with
regulations for daily life, God's great design is destroyed by
man's small mind. Regulations may be necessary, but
many of them are simply irrelevant for the kingdom.

Religious obedience is the insertion of a person in a
specific way into the design of God for the visible Church.
Authority is conferred on a superior in such a way that he
has to leave a large field for the initiative and creative
talents of the members of the community. If he does not,
but overwhelms them with laws and rules, he is not fulfilling God's design, but acting outside it. He would be
bringing his community back to the slavery of the law
instead of respecting the freedom they received from
Christ.

Obedience conceived in this way is based on faith in
the visible Church. It means dedication to the work of
Christ through a faithful response to the command that
comes from those to whom authority was given. But those
who command have to serve the kingdom and should not
shift the emphasis in their commands to small human
things. They are duty bound to respect the freedom of
God's children acquired at such a great price by Christ.
Then obedience appears as the liberation of the person: he

accepts the authority of the Church and uses all his gifts and talents to help the expansion of the kingdom among all men.

A final text from the Decree gives some indication of the hidden strength of Christ which is present in genuine religious obedience:

> Therefore, in a spirit of faith and of love for God's will, let religious show humble obedience to their superiors in accord with the norms of rule and constitution (Abbott, *op cit.*, p. 476).

The norms of rule and constitution, however good or holy, have a subsidiary role to play. The rule of life for any religious as for any Christian is to follow the guidance of the Holy Spirit. Such a guidance will not destroy the external embodiment of the spirit of the institute in the norms, but may well go beyond them. If the norms are open, no real problem is likely to arise. If they are closed, the sooner they are revised the better, for if they are not they may become an impediment to the inspirations of the Holy Spirit.

The word of God and the need to bring it alive in the life of the community and the individual religious takes priority over any written rules. This is simply to say with the Council that the Gospel is to be regarded as the supreme law of religious life. Nothing ever can be sacrificed to charity, and if an apparent conflict arises between the demands of Christian love and the written rule, charity has absolute precedence. Even if there is a doubt, the decision should favor the theological virtue of charity, not the security of a man-made regulation.

It may be useful to note, also, that the expression that a person takes his vows "to the constitutions" can be falsely interpreted. The written documents are no more than an expression of a living body and spirit, a partial image of the internal riches of the community. The vows are really not taken "to the constitutions" but to a living body. Religious vows are promises of fidelity and service to the universal Church, and in the Church to a particular community. Therefore the person who takes the vows is bound to the living community that changes and develops according to the laws of a living being. Changes in the constitutions can, accordingly, be binding even if they are made after a person has taken his vows, for he vowed fidelity and service to a living body, not to written works.

5

God's Trusteeship: Government

The documents published by the Council are marked by a deep vision of unity. The Church is not considered in isolation, but in its union with the whole human race. Catholics are no longer seen as segregated from other Christians, but as one with them, in spite of real differences. The pope and the bishops form one organic body in the episcopal college.

The same vision of unity is extended to religious institutes. In them the head and the members form one body, and the healthy life of the community depends on a balanced collaboration. This is why the problems of government and obedience cannot be separated: they are two aspects of the functioning of the same organic body. If either of them is infected, the whole body suffers. However, it is still practical to consider separately the problems attaching to government and obedience. Our concern here is with government, according to the mind of the Council as expressed in the Decree on the renewal and adaptation of the religious life to modern times, even though for the sake of balance, we shall have to refer occasionally to the question of obedience. The Council provides us with a new vision of government in religious life. Not, of course, in the sense that it changes the substance of the tradition inherited from such masters as St. Benedict, St. Francis of Assisi or St. Ignatius of Loyola, but that it gives us a better understanding of God's plan for men and women called to live under the guidance of a religious superior.

The new vision that the Council's teaching provides is the unity of a religious body or community, and the understanding that a closer relationship between the head and the members, far from destroying the authority of the head, actually strengthens it.

In order to give an account of this new insight that the Council affords, and to explain its content, it will be necessary to say something of the antecedents of the Council: how the work of theologians laid the foundation for a better understanding of the life of a religious community. Then we shall examine those documents of the Council which treat of government in the Church in general, and the Decree, *Perfectae Caritatis,* in particular, which deals with government in religious life. This will be followed by an attempt at a short theological synthesis, in which the harmony and the balance of the Council's doctrine can be better seen; and by way of conclusion, we shall offer some practical applications and considerations.

HISTORICAL BACKGROUND

One of the signs of the divine origin of the Church is the harmonious balance in her life of seemingly contradicting qualities, such as stability and openness to change. This balance can never be completely destroyed, since it is the work of the Spirit of Christ. But it can be upset by our own lack of understanding. In recent centuries there has been so much stress on the permanent elements in the life of the Church, that in her practical living full play has not always been granted to the inspiration of the Spirit. Our liturgy reflected the permanent beauty of God, but not the powerful wind and the tongues of fire of the Holy Spirit. Similarly, our conception of government in the Church affirmed the permanent presence of God through legitimate authority, but perhaps it failed to give due weight to the less articulate and less tangible presence of the Spirit in every member of the social body. To enter into the mind of the Council, we must accept both these principles: that is, to stand firmly on the rock which is immovable and to be exposed fully to the wind of the Spirit who moves us. The old tradition has to be blended with a new inspiration.

What then are the principal developments in theology which seem relevant for religious government and obedience?

The Development of the Doctrine of the Mystical Body. This development has provided us with a better understanding of the structure and the life of the Church. The Pauline image of the Church as an organic body has emerged into the full light of day. Head and members are no longer considered as separate units, but as the organs of one body. The realization that the organs are held together by the Spirit of Christ has deepened. Since the one Spirit lives in many members, there is an invisible communication among them; no single one of them could live without the others. The dynamic quality of the life of the mystical body has also been emphasized. It has been discovered anew how the Spirit of God infuses life and movement into the whole Church and into the smallest part of it, with the practical conclusion that this life must be made manifest by new initiatives, which reflect the dynamic presence of the Spirit in the whole community.

Development in the Vision of Authority. Following on this more profound understanding of the mystery of the Church, it was rediscovered (if this term is legitimate in theology) that the highest form of authority in the Church in its deepest reality is of a collegiate nature: not in a legal, but in a theological sense, whereby college means communion and organic union. However, this communion of many in the one power of Christ has a hierarchical structure: the position of the head and his share in the power of Christ is different from that of the members. But the close union between the head and the members, that is, between the pope and the bishops, does not destroy the full authority of the head; rather it strengthens it. This general vision of authority has been incorporated, in an analogous form, in the Decree on religious life.

New Insight into the Function of Authority. Authority has increasingly come to be understood as service. The legal element in exercising power is being reduced to its right proportion, and a more spiritual image of the superior is emerging: the servant of the people of God, whether in a large community, or in a small one. The type of this service is not that of the Roman slave, but of Christ the servant of Yahweh, who received his authority primarily from the Spirit dwelling in him. He taught with power, he promulgated the law of the new covenant; but he also washed the feet of his disciples, and served them with a hot breakfast on a cold morning on the shore of the Lake of Tiberias. He himself summed up the qualities of this good servant when he described the good shepherd who leads the flock, feeds the flock and gives his life for it: a complex biblical image that cannot be fitted into any legal scheme. Some of the old names for religious superiors contain this scriptural idea: abbot means father and minister means servant. This is not to deny that the spiritual power of the superior needs a legal framework to support it: the invisible and divine element must be embodied in a visible and human organization.

Infallibility Cannot Be Delegated.   If there was ever a tendency to suggest or to insinuate that some sort of infallibility is attached to offices not instituted by Christ, such as to the office of a religious superior who is not a bishop or does not share the episcopal power in some other way, it has certainly come to an end. All agree that infallibility cannot be delegated. Apart from the supreme authority functioning in special circumstances, for example, the pope or council in defining doctrinal questions, all other authorities in the Church are subject to human failure, and there are bound to be mistakes in their judgments and actions. It follows that, in order to understand the mystery of government and obedience in religious life, we have to look in the Church towards that field of human activity where persons holding an office, although helped by the Spirit, are subject to failure, and not towards the field of divine guarantees that exempt the highest authority from error.

Development of the Theology of the Divine Indwelling.   Nowadays, more account is taken of the invisible capabilities of a child of God which follow from the presence of the Spirit; his inspirations and desires can be better discerned and a greater scope can be given to them.

At the same time, the social nature of God's grace has been further explored, and we realize better that the grace God wants to give a community will somehow be given through all the members—even as the fullness of life is given to our body through all its organs. If communication between the members breaks down, or the graces and gifts offered to individuals are not valued, the whole body will be poorer for it, and it may even become sick, manifesting all the symptoms of spiritual malnutrition.

These theological trends converged at the Council and produced abundant fruit in its constitutions, decrees, and declarations.

THE COUNCIL

The Decree on religious life is not an isolated pronouncement. Its true sense cannot be grasped and appreciated unless it is considered in the context of the other documents. The idea of government in religious life is hardly more than an application of the idea of authority in the Church to the particular case of religious. Even within the field of religious life it will take different forms and shades, according to the personality of each institute. The Council does not want to destroy diversity, but to inspire in religious a common element of universality.

The Constitution on the Church, *Lumen Gentium,* explains in detail the nature of the supreme power that is present within the communion of bishops, with the pope as their head. This power and authority is owned by a communion of persons, although its exercise belongs either to the pope alone, or to the college—which can only move with the consent of the head. This is not strictly the case in a religious institute, but an important analogy remains. The close union of the members with the head, even to the extent of the members taking an active part in the deliberations of the institute, does not destroy the authority of the head, but confirms it. A body is not weaker because the head and members work closely together.

According to the same constitution, laymen are to be caught up into the life of the Church to a degree rarely envisaged in recent times. They should be consulted, trusted, and given an active part in the life of the universal Church, the diocese, and the parish. They should have a freedom of action, and their wishes and desires should be considered with due attention. Here again the dominant note of unity is sounded: the flock and the shepherd should be one. But the roles are not reversed: the flock cannot have any legal power over the shepherd.

The Decree on the life and ministry of priests, *Presbyterorum Ordinis,* directs that the bishops should see in their priests their brothers and friends. They all share the one priesthood of Christ, even if not to the same extent; the bishop has the fullness of it, the priests a lesser share. The Council recommends that a senate of priests be instituted in every diocese to assist the bishop and to express the unity of the priesthood. On a lesser scale the college of priests surrounding the bishop is parallel to the college of bishops surrounding the pope. The desire of the Church is that the legitimate power of the bishop, which always remains his, should be exercised within the context of this spiritual and practical communion between the bishop and his priests.

All these cases offer us an analogy which clarifies the meaning of our Decree when it speaks of religious government. The theme of unity between the head and the members will dominate.

Perhaps the best way of penetrating into the inner meaning of the Decree, *Perfectæ Caritatis,* is to take some of its leading ideas on government as they are expressed in n. 14 and to explain them in a theological context (Abbott, *op. cit.,* 476–7).

Superiors have the souls of their subjects entrusted to them. In other words, superiors are God's trustees, with the right and duty to protect and help the souls of their subjects. Let us beware of any sort of platonism: soul here means the whole person who is a child of God with an eternal destiny. A trustee is not an owner: he has to administer the property of another, according to the wishes of the one who commissioned him. The somewhat legal concept of trusteeship in this case becomes profoundly theological: the superior is not the owner of the subject, but has to take care of him in the name of another: Christ in this case. It follows that the personality of the trustee has to withdraw to a healthy degree so that Christ's personality should have a free impact on the subject. A superior should never try to transform a community to his own ideals; he should have the humility to hide himself, and let Christ impress his own image on them. This will give stability to every religious community; the change of superior will not mean a radical change of outlook and way of life. At the same time, the superior should keep all his legitimate power: no good trustee would allow it to be denied or destroyed.

"Each superior should himself be docile to God's will in the exercise of his office." Here we touch a crucial point. To be docile means to be open, to be ready to receive new knowledge. It also means a readiness of will to put the knowledge into practice.

Docility to the will of God signifies a devoted search to know this will, and a selfless determination to carry it out. Therefore the Decree assumes that the will of God frequently exists and can be known prior to the decision of the superior, at least in substance. Otherwise the text would be meaningless. It follows that the substance of the office of the superior is to obey; to obey the will of God, and to put great effort in trying to know it, to formulate it and to specify it for his subjects. This general will of God, antecedent to any decision by the superior can be known by reading the signs of the times, by looking for God's designs in the ordinary events of his providence. It can also be known through the inspirations of the Holy Spirit. Either of these means of knowing the will of God, that is, reading God's design in events and discovering his will through inspirations, is open to the superior and to his subjects. The search for the will of God should therefore be a concerted effort of the community; without a continuous and honest dialog (not reduced to a mere formality) between the superior and the subjects, the will of God simply cannot be known adequately. This dialog should not be restricted to spiritual matters. It should extend to all practical problems of the subject's life: his assignment to various jobs, and all the human problems of his external apostolate.

But in the last analysis, it is the superior who must make the binding decision. If he is docile, he is likely to set the real will of God as the norm of action for his subjects; but if he is not open in his heart, he may fail to do so. Yet provided the subject does not deliberately cooperate in a sinful order, he will be protected supernaturally in carrying our the mistaken order, since "we know God cooperates with those who love him" (Rom 8, 28). Nonetheless, the failure of the superior to conform in his order to the pattern of the will of God will have a disrupting effect on the life of the community. There is no divine guarantee that all orders will serve to the greatest good of the institution in question. Bad government can do untold harm to it, even if obedience is perfect. The history of religious orders and congregations offers abundant proof of this.

A fundamental quality in a good superior is an unlimited capacity to listen. God's creative activity is taking place around him: in events, in his own mind and heart, and in those of every member of the community. To neglect to listen to any one of them may well mean that the superior cuts himself off from information that God wants him to have. It would be a failure in docility, with disastrous effects for the community, if the case is a serious one.

"Let him use his authority in a spirit of service for the brethren, and manifest thereby the charity with which God loves them." We have already seen that the evangelical concept of service is complex and includes both authority and humble care for the spiritual and temporal needs of the subject. It certainly includes a humble mind and a real living devotion towards the religious, who are the chosen children of God. It must include humble actions, analogous to those performed by servants. Otherwise the humble mind is not expressed: the word does not take on flesh. A superior who is not inclined to consider those under his care as his friends, equals, and even his superiors in the Spirit, is certainly not a person after the heart of Christ, the servant of Yahweh.

In their government, superiors should express the love of God for his children (Abbott, *op. cit.*, p. 477). The room for comment here is unlimited, but one quality that is certainly the manifestation of God's love is to trust another person.

The trust that the superior has in his subjects should resemble the trust that God has in us. He has every reason to distrust us: he has been more than once deceived by our lack of fidelity. We have all abused his goodness. Nevertheless, his confidence in his children remains unshaken. He is always ready to grant his pardon. And when he forgives our trespasses, he also forgets them, and we can start again with the generous capital of God's good will. The life of a good religious can be made unjustly hard because of a fault once committed, and never really forgiven, or, if forgiven, never forgotten. True love covers up everything, and always concedes a fresh start: not seven times, but seventy times seven.

There is no policy nor pedagogical device which can bring so much out of a person of good will as the conviction that he is trusted. It must be taken for granted, of course, that not all persons will be of good will and that our trust will be abused by some, in the same way as the good will of God is sometimes abused. But better isolated abuses than the steady abuse of God's love by lack of trust. To avoid any misunderstanding, let us say clearly that Christian trust never excludes legitimate prudence. Lack of trust is lack of charity: prudence is the expression of real charity.

"Governing his subjects as God's own sons, and with regard for their human personality, a superior will make it easier for them to obey gladly." Here it may be useful to say something about the difference between the external and the internal aspect of the Church. The external aspect is the hierarchical visible structure. It is based on the mysterious power to govern that Christ has handed over to the apostles, and which arises from the nature of an organized society. It is essentially temporal and connected with a legal framework. The internal aspect is the union of the faithful with Christ through his Spirit, a union that is invisible. It is eternal, since it consists in the possession of the best of all charisms, charity. Now the superior's office belongs to the external aspect of the Church; the perfection of each one in charity belongs to its internal structure. Externally, there is a hierarchy of authority; internally, there is a hierarchy of charity. The two do not necessarily coincide. Though the superior is in a higher position within the visible framework of the community, many of his subjects may be in a higher position in the intensity and purity of their charity. A delicate and practical balance of mutual respect is needed here: while the subject must acknowledge Christ's public authority in the superior, the superior must revere and be aware of the invisible authority of the Spirit of God present in his subjects.

It is God's will that each of his children should reflect his glory in a way that is absolutely unique. Therefore the superior should take care that the particular gifts of grace given to each person should develop, as his own special grace should develop too. Any attempt to standardize devotions and attitudes over and above the common heritage of the institute is harmful to the community.

It may be useful to recall that there cannot be a real growth in spiritual life if a certain margin is not left for the inevitable mistakes and faults. Men and women do not enter religious life because they are perfect but because they want to mature in God's love. Now any process of growth and development in a person is tied up with mistakes and failures. If a climate is created where the slightest false step is reproached and harshly corrected, the members of the community may take refuge consciously or unconsciously in a spiritual immobility. If a person does not move, he will not make mistakes. But he will not mature either: he may remain an apparently disciplined person, but not a creative child of God.

To be a human personality is to be unique, somehow similar to God. To be a human person is to have one's own mind and heart, a personal vision of the world and a basic freedom to act. To respect a person means to respect his uniqueness, his talents, and all that is good in him, in his opinions and in his desires. This respect does not mean that those personal gifts cannot be sacrificed to some extent for God's sake, or that they cannot be given a new direction when necessary; but it does mean an essentially humble attitude towards the individual and the sincere intention to help him to remain a person, unique in this creation. We have to remember that to destroy a human personality means to destroy a particular and irreplaceable reflection of God's glory in this created world. Again, in the context of incorporation into the mystical body and of religious profession, each one is given a special power to contribute all that is his unique personal possession, so that Christ himself can live in him, and develop those human possibilities which he could not himself develop in his own single individual human nature. This is why the superior has to consider all the qualities of the subjects concerned when he is making a decision. He is God's steward, and will have to give an account of every single talent that God has given, not only to himself, but also to his subjects. For both, the reckoning will still be exacting, as it is described in the parable of the talents (Mt 25, 14–30).

To respect a man or woman as a person means to respect his mind. When a decision is communicated or an order given to a subject, it is the superior's duty in charity (though not in law) to give him as much information about the order as is reasonably possible, so that the subject should not remain in obscurity, but should participate fully in the work suggested or requested. In this way the dignity of the human person is preserved; and the result will be a much more efficient work and a much closer tie between the head and the members. A wise superior will not try to keep his subjects in an intellectual vacuum, but will integrate their minds into the common work of the whole institute. In this way he will greatly contribute to the intelligent praise that every religious body has to offer to God.

To respect a human person means also to leave him a certain amount of freedom. Rules are meant to be a framework to help the individuals and the community to create the most helpful climate for the work of the Holy Spirit. One can have too few rules, and the result will be chaos. One can have too many rules, and the result will be a burden that destroys the freshness of mind and heart so necessary to receive the inspirations of the Spirit. If no reasonable amount of freedom is left for each person, the spirit of prophecy (which should exist in every Christian community to a greater or lesser degree) will be soon destroyed.

There cannot be a real respect for a human person if his personal maturity is not respected. Each religious should be treated according to his own age and mental capacity. Novices between the age of eighteen and twenty should not be treated as if they were much younger, and the novitiate should not have the air of a school for children. Grown-up men and women in religious communities should have all the consideration that is due to an adult person. They should have a more generous allowance of freedom within the substantial framework of the rule.

The Council insists in particular on the freedom due to religious in the matter of confession and spiritual direction. The consequence of this insistence may well be the relaxation of the law of special faculties for nuns. It would be a welcome change. Perhaps the insistence of the Council will help also to remove the last traces of well-meant but ill-conceived restrictions, which may exist still here and there, more in actual practice than in any written rule.

Superiors are enjoined to promote in their subjects the virtue of active and responsible obedience: "Let [them] give the kind of friendship which will encourage religious to bring an active and responsible obedience to the offices they shoulder and the activities they undertake."

A human person cannot be active, unless he expresses himself in a personal and creative way. And the Council is saying that religious obedience cannot be perfect unless it includes this personal and creative element, both in new initiatives and in bringing to fulfillment works already begun. The ideal of obedience is not in an ever increasing passivity, but in the right blend of the essential dependence on the will of the superior and a personal and creative contribution towards the goal intended. Great scope is given by the Council to the inspirations of the subject and to his talents and gifts, but they have to be used within the framework laid down by the legitimate authority.

Activity supposes and entails responsibility. A responsible person is able to foresee the probable consequences of his acts; he takes them into account in planning his actions, and recognizes that he must answer for them. He is also a trustworthy person: important jobs can be given him; and it is anticipated that he will have the capacity to solve a complex question in a balanced way without over-simplifying it. Responsibility represents an intellectual element in the person, an ability to weigh reasons for what they are worth without being unduly affected emotionally.

The mark of wise government, according to the mind of the Council, is the good judgment of the superior which blends orders with a proper allowance for freedom in his subjects. A discerning superior will find a balance between imposing his own will on another person and letting him formulate a responsible decision. Virtue does not lie in either of the extremes. It does not lie in a passivity which makes one await prompting from above for every action, nor in a fully independent activity either, which would destroy the submission essential for any true obedience.

The perfection of active and responsible obedience cannot be reached in a day. An understanding superior will know that the persons entrusted to him will learn it by trial and error. To promote this Christian obedience, "a superior should listen willingly to his subjects." They will certainly talk if a climate of confidence is established within the community.

For this climate of mutual trust, it is essential to know that secrets of conscience are scrupulously respected. By the law of the Church no religious has an obligation to manifest his conscience to his superior. If he does so, he hands over his own private property and has a right to ask that it should not become public. The local superior is not entitled to pass on any knowledge concerning the conscience of a person to a higher official, for any reason what-ever, unless he has the explicit permission of the person concerned, a permission which is not to be requested lightly, is never presumed, and is invalid if it is obtained with subtle constraint. The absolute respect for this law, and the knowledge that its breach is never tolerated, will help younger persons to seek help from their immediate superiors. In this way vocations can be strengthened or saved; problems will come before the superior in good time. Obviously, it is permitted to a local superior to suggest that the subject himself should seek help from a higher superior, provided the suggestion does not curtail the person's freedom.

No one should ever be blamed for having ideas and inspirations when he communicates them to the superior. Even if the subject were to say the wrong thing, he would be saying it to the right person and in the right place, where slanted visions and ill-conceived projects can be corrected.

The superior should distinguish and separate the field of conscience from the field of external administration. No advantage should be taken of a confidential communication between the superior and the subject in imposing external discipline.

Perhaps we ought to mention how necessary it is for a superior to have a wide Christian and human culture. If he does not have it, he will be inclined to silence a person when he should be discussing his problems. If he has this culture, he will be able to enter into a real dialogue.

The Council wants the cooperation of all the members for the good of the institute: the superior should "encourage them to make a personal contribution to the welfare of the community."

This cooperation is not possible unless all members

are integrated in the right way into the life of the community. This integration supposes a fair amount of information about the work and the problems of the whole institute. A wise superior will know how much to say about the financial situation of the house, the projects for the future, the successes and failures in the past, in order to create that family spirit which makes each one feel responsible for the others and for the good of the whole body. Complete silence about these topics will not promote cooperation. It is not an answer to say that the ordinary members of the community have no right to know the secrets of administration. They may not have a legal right, granted, but the true charity of the superior will cover this lack of a right, and will not leave them in the dark.

At the same time, the Council makes it clear that the right to make a final decision and to give an order belongs to the superior. The new provisions in the Decree do not destroy the basic concept of authority. They are meant to strengthen it.

The union between the head and the members of religious communities is expressed especially through the work of the chapters and councils. Their job is to help the superior with independent judgments. The final verdict will have to come from the authoritative source, but before it is given, the advisers have to speak their own mind without any human regard. But once the decision has been taken, they, too, have to obey.

Through the work of the chapter and the councils, all the members of the institute should somehow cooperate for the good of the whole body. This provision implies that the composition of these groups should be representative to a reasonable degree. If they are not, the institute should revise its constitutions. A chapter in which the majority of the members is appointed by a higher superior (directly or indirectly) and only a minority elected, would not correspond to the ideals of Vatican Council II.

It was not the intention of the Council to give an exhaustive description of the office of the superior, but to state some essential principles which would help the life of the community and promote the right type of obedience. At the same time, the Council wished to stress certain points on which the prevailing doctrine or practice of government needed gentle correction. Therefore the content of the Decree must be put into a broader theological context; otherwise there might be an unbalanced presentation of it.

In the Church, there are offices of divine institution with a charism attached to them. Such are the priestly offices in their various degrees. The pope, the bishops, and the priests are all in possession of an office to the holder of which a special assistance of the Holy Spirit is guaranteed. This assistance is not easily explained in theological terms, since it is part of the mystery of the Church. But the assistance is there independently of the worthiness of the person; it is there because of the office. By God's will it is given to the person through the office and not otherwise.

The theological status of a religious superior is situated at a different level. There is no particular charism attached to his office; the office is not conferred sacramentally. The superior does not have a grace of office in the strict sense, as bishops have it, but he is personally assisted by God, as every good Christian is, to fulfill the task that God gives him. So, the graces the religious superior re-

ceives are given to him not through his office, but personally, in view of the fact that he has to govern. God assists
the superior in his government, as God assists the subject
in his obedience. From this assistance it would be no more
legitimate to conclude that the superior governs in the
right way than it would be legitimate to conclude that the
subject obeys in the right way.

To clarify the theological elements of the office of the
superior means to discover in it God's gracious mystery:
through the superior, God is working out the plans of his
providence, a divine action is taking place in a human
context.

This context does not include a special charism attached to the office, either in the form of infallibility in
judging an issue, or in the form of unfailing prudence in
practical deeds. The superior's judgments are fallible and
his prudence subject to failures.

At the same time, these human elements are in a divine context. Here faith in providence comes in. The
world is governed by God, and he takes care of his chosen
ones through the fragile actions of a human person. This
faith in the providence of God is the answer to the doubts
and anxieties arising from the human limitations of a superior. Through a human person God is working towards
achieving his plan of love with regard to the superior himself, and to his subjects. The perfection of the superior's
judgments and actions is not divinely guaranteed, but
God's effective love towards all *is* guaranteed.

It is vital that the superior should be well aware of his
own theological position, of the graces that he may or may
not have. Any miscalculation would result in taking a
wrong direction in government, while the knowledge of
the truth will have a liberating effect on him and his com-

munity, and will help them all to use the available resources fully.

Since there is no charism attached to the office by divine law, it follows that the personal qualities (natural and
supernatural) of the superior will have the greatest importance. If he is closely united to God, he is likely to discern
God's will in the external events and the internal inspirations; then he will be able to formulate it or specify it for
his subjects, and lead the whole community to God.

The need for this spiritual vision in the superior is
evident: without it he will never reach the necessary degree of discernment. The necessity of some training on a
human level is equally important. Here, the science of
human relations can prove helpful, and a knowledge of
psychology almost indispensable. A fair amount of human
culture is more than useful; without it a dialogue with the
community, and the consideration of new ideas, is hardly
possible. Openness of mind and heart is essential; the Holy
Spirit cannot work through those whose minds are closed
to a new wind, to new tongues of fire, and to persons
speaking a new language.

The knowledge by the superior of his own theological
position is bound to have a double effect. First, it will
inspire in him a deep sense of humility. He will know that
his decisions are not infallibly right. This awareness of his
own limitations will make him eager to intensify his own
relationship with God, because he has to be the interpreter
of God's will. It will also make him open to suggestions
before a decision is taken, and to a reasonable amount of
open discussion after the decision has been made. A good
superior will know that he may have made a mistake, and
the subject who represents his own view may bring him a
new light. Therefore, he will receive the subject with

humility, leaving the door open for the correction of his decision, either by himself or by a higher authority. Precisely because the immediate superior can make a mistake in interpreting or specifying the will of God, there ought to be a margin of security in going to higher superiors. But when the point is reached where, considering the importance of the case, it would be unreasonable to go further in discussions or appeals, it is to be assumed that God's providence works through the order received. No further move should be made. The competent superior should decree the case closed, and the subject should obey with simplicity.

Second, this theological knowledge will give the superior a sense of security. He will not have to claim that his decision is the only correct one. He can rightly ask for obedience even in the case of an imperfect decision, because God's mystery will still be present in it.

This sense of security will be reenforced by the fact that a humble superior will not lean on his own wisdom alone: his open-mindedness will make him gather the best of reasons from every source. He will have the accumulated wisdom of his brethren. At the same time he will know that he has authority, and will not be afraid to use it. He will know that he has a right to bind and to loose (in the broad sense of the term) in the name of Christ. He is the chosen instrument of God's providence.

To complete the picture, it may be well to recall that a divine guarantee of protection exists only for the salvation and spiritual good of a person, and not for the life and development of a religious institute. Bad administration can harm a religious community slightly, or seriously, or even fatally. This statement is valid even when the superior acts in good faith, but in an inefficient way. The institute will inevitably be harmed, although the souls of the superior and subject will be saved. One of the alarming signs will be the lack of vocations. The evil state of the world should not be blamed for lack of vocations; a serious examination of conscience should be held by the religious body concerned. God has his chosen ones in every age and at every place; but he will not inspire them to join an organization which is not in harmony with his plans.

It is also well to recall that there is no divine guarantee that the human values of a subject will be safeguarded in the case of mistakes in government, even if the mistakes are made in good faith. A nervous breakdown may have its cause in misguided orders coming from above, though there is, of course, a guarantee that the breakdown will serve for the spiritual good of the suffering person.

In religious government which functions according to the mind of Christ, the mystery of incarnation is present. God comes through human words and actions to redeem us from ourselves and give us his own life. In this process, the superior plays the part of the human steward for the divine Master. The ideal is that he should reflect in himself the image of Christ.

SOME PRACTICAL POINTS

There is no good government without an honest respect for the so-called principle of subsidiarity. This principle enunciates a law valid for any society or community, and can be stated in various ways: "A superior organ should never take over the function of an inferior one, but should only subsidize its strength when it is necessary." Or, "Every organ in a body should function to its full capacity." Or, less technically: "Each person should be left to do his job fully: his superior should not interfere unless the common good imposes it." The practical applications are numerous, but some examples can be given. The work of a headmaster should not be taken over fully or partially by his superior if the two offices are given to distinct persons; the priest who is in charge of a community of lay brothers should not dictate each separate item of the daily menu to the cook, and so on.

Respect for facts is another mark of wise government. To dissociate oneself from facts means to cut oneself off from the living source of the will of God. Therefore if there are problems in a community, they should not be swept under the carpet, but faced with robust realism. The more one enters into the real world of God, the more one is united with God's plans.

Fear and apprehension are rarely good counsels for prudent decisions. A Christian should be able to listen to anything, to hear any idea, because he has the discernment to choose what is good, and to leave aside what is bad. Fear may cause a complex which compels the superior to silence persons with new or unusual ideas, without giving them an answer. The ideas, of course, will not be suppressed. They will go underground and will do far more harm than if they had been allowed to be aired and then answered properly, either by the superior or perhaps by someone else who can do so.

A superior who wants to help his subjects to love God will know how to discourage servility. Servile obedience tends to concentrate on the human qualities of the superior, and tries to obtain favors through misguided signs of respect. A climate against servility can be built up if it is known that the superior appreciates those who are ready to tell the truth as they see it. If, on the contrary, it is felt in the community that the opinions of those who agree in everything with the ideas of the superior are the most highly esteemed, then the strength of the community will be undermined.

Finally, the mark of a good superior is that in him seemingly opposing qualities appear in harmony. He is the servant of all, and yet he knows how to lead. He wants to preserve what is precious in the traditions and yet he is eager to receive new inspirations. He has a broad vision, and yet he is practical when action and help are needed. He is with God and he is also fully with his fellow-members in the community.

6

Earthly Wisdom in the Kingdom: Government

Government in religious life is frequently understood as the function and activity of the superior of a local community or of the major superior, be he the head of a province or of a whole institute. This is, however, an undue restriction of the concept of government, which entails a far more complex and extensive activity in which the superiors have an eminent, but by no means exclusive, place.

Government means leading the whole community towards the kingdom of God, freeing the whole community from all encumbrances so that it can be fully open to the impact of the Spirit of God, coordinating all graces and gifts the community possesses. It means also a religious respect for every person in the community. This complex activity requires legislation, execution of the laws, and arbitration when it is necessary. There must be legislation: general norms must be given to the whole institute. These norms should act as main directives, clear guide lines, as well as a liberating force that achieves a deep union with the Spirit. They should be a source of unity with respect for diversity. Further, there should be organs in the community that are in charge of executing these laws; their concern should be the application, not the making of the laws. Finally, there should be some judicial organ in every institute to resolve doubts about the interpretation of laws and to redress injustices if and when they occur. Because every community is human, it is to be expected that there will be doubts about the meaning of laws, conflicting interpretations of the constitutions, and, sometimes, unintended or even intentional injustices. Every community therefore needs some sort of machinery to resolve doubts and conflicts and to examine complaints and grievances. In the technical language of jurisprudence we speak about the legislative, executive, and judicial branches of power. No human community should be deprived of the wisdom that has devised this division of power into three branches. Experience proves abundantly that the life of a community is happier and more balanced, and its work more efficient if the *one* power is divided among *three* organs. Such a division is not an invasion of politics into religious life. The division existed in religious life long before it was adopted by modern political philosophy.

LEGISLATIVE POWER IN RELIGIOUS LIFE

The problems concerning legislative power in religious life can be considered under three headings: the problem of representation—who should be the legislators? the problem of the openness of the legislative body to the Holy Spirit, to the needs of the world, and of the institute —how can new laws be promptly provided for new needs? the problem of establishing guiding principles for legislation—how are wise laws made?

The Composition of the Legislative Body. The Council decree states that renewal should be the common work of the whole religious institute. It states further that this work of renewal cannot be done once for all; it has to be continuous. The chief instrument of the renewal is the legislative body of the institute, the general chapter. Since the chapter acts in the name of the whole institute, in some way it must represent the best aspirations of the community as a whole and of the individual members. In other words, the chapter must have a representation of both quality and quantity. In every institute there are members or small groups blessed with special graces, talents, or experience. It is fitting that these exceptional gifts should be somehow present within the legislative body. Moreover, in every institute there is a basic equality among all the members that does not depend on personal qualities; it is therefore fitting that all the members should be somehow represented. A wise balance in the composition of the chapter will accordingly be reached when there is a balance of quality and quantity. A system of representation based merely on the majority of votes would not necessarily bring out the best in the community. It could lead to the spiritual and material impoverishment of the institute if the majority of the members are not well informed or well inspired. Another system of representation based on quality alone could easily lead to the domination of the institute by one group representing one school of thought and not a variety of graces. In the past, this problem of quality and quantity representation was resolved by giving the right to attend to those who held major administrative offices in an institute, and admitting, also, a certain number of delegates freely elected, either by direct vote of the members or by a smaller body of electors chosen by the direct vote of the members.

No chapter can be truly representative of the institute unless about two-thirds of the chapter-members are freely elected, and no more than about one-third enter the chapter by right of office. If such a proportion is not preserved, a dangerous situation can develop. If those who enter the general chapter by right of office are in the majority, or are present in such numbers that they can impede any motion contrary to their ideas, then *one* school of thought, *one* interpretation of the traditions, *one* vision of the future will be perpetuated. The spirit of an institute is much richer than the vision and interpretation of one group in it. If one group of superiors is able to impose its ideas and administrative ways on the general chapter and on the institute (by appointing persons of the same mind as local superiors) gradually the institute would lose its riches, probably a number of vocations, would be subject to one-sided leadership, and would not grow healthily and vigorously. Those who enter the chapter by election should be able to change the whole administration if they judge it necessary for the good of the institute.

With the expansion and growth of an institute a new problem may emerge: the great number of representatives at the general chapter. If there are many provinces, many provincials will attend the chapter, and for each provincial there should be two freely elected delegates. The result may well be that the chapter becomes an unwieldy legislative instrument. The solution is simple in theory and difficult in practice: the number of members of the chapter must be reduced without sacrificing any of the principles of representation explained earlier. This can be done in many ways, for example, by admitting only some of the provincial superiors to the chapter (perhaps by election) , and having two delegates elected for each provincial. Such elections could be made on a regional basis.

The possibility of electing representatives on the basis of the different types of work the institute is engaged in should be explored. For instance, if the institute operates high schools, the principals of these schools could elect a representative, and so for those institutes that run hospitals, or parishes. This leads to another question: could the general chapter be divided into two chambers? One would consist of superiors (one-third) and freely elected members on a territorial basis (two-thirds) ; the other would be composed of eminent specialists appointed partly by the superiors (one-third), partly by election by their peers (two-thirds) . The size of both chambers should be kept reasonably small, and for the passing of the laws the consent of both groups would be necessary, with the proviso that, in case of a disagreement, after attempts at conciliation, the opinion of the territorial chamber should prevail.

Is such an idea realistic and practical? There are certainly good elements in it, but it is untried. It is not definitely advocated here, but proposed to stimulate research. Should we not explore *all* alternatives in order to select the best?

Openness to the Spirit and to the Needs of the World. The very essence of religious life is that the members have the spiritual mission of the prophets, in the sense that they have been charged by God to transmit a message to his people. By accepting their vocation of virginity, poverty, and obedience to the Church in a community, they let the word of God come alive in themselves. They preach that "the kingdom is at hand," even before they say a word; but they have to announce it by word of mouth as well—and this is prophetic activity. The source of this mission is the Holy Spirit: he gives it, he keeps it alive. Now, such a vocation cannot be fulfilled unless the religious institute as a whole, and its members as individuals, are continuously open to the Spirit: he it is who gives the message. At the same time, institutes and individuals have to be aware of the needs of the world: the world has to receive the message. Obviously, such a vocation cannot be fulfilled unless there is openness in both directions, toward God and toward the world. It cannot exist in the life of an institute unless it is present in their legislative body, that is, in their general chapter. Openness means listening to the Holy Spirit; and it means watching for the signs of the times in the world.

A practical conclusion follows: a general chapter that is convoked rarely and perhaps with little preparation cannot have this openness. An institute in which the supreme legislative power does not function except once every six or nine years, for some two or three months, cannot keep up with the inspiration of the Spirit for a fast-moving world, or with the needs of the Church in this modern world. Such a system may have been useful in the past; it is not satisfactory at present. Yet, most religious institutes have an anachronistic way of convoking and celebrating their general chapter; only a few, if any, have the machinery for quick and efficient legislation. No wonder many communities fall behind their time. The solution toward a new openness may well lie in more frequent convocations of the general chapter—provided, of course, that the numbers of those taking part are kept reasonably low. A general chapter every two years may well be necessary today in order to make major policy decisions and establish new laws for new needs.

There could, however, be an intermediate solution to this problem: The general chapter, after having laid down the main lines of legislation, could elect a standing committee whose duty would be to keep working after the general chapter is dissolved and to fill in the details of legislation. The very same committee could also prepare the next general chapter. In this way there would be steady legislative activity in the institute. The upheaval that chapters convoked every six or nine years are bound to cause would become a thing of the past. Anyone in the institute who has a proposition for future legislation would be allowed to approach the committee at any time. Needless to say, such a committee would be a legislative organ, part of, and subject to, the general chapter and, as far as legislation or its preparation is concerned, not subject to the general superior. To avoid any conflict in practice, the general superior or his delegate could be the committee's chairman.

A living legislative body functioning with continuity would be the best instrument of openness to both the inspirations of the Spirit and the needs of the world.

The Spirit of Laws. The legislative power will function best if the members of the chapter keep in mind that their vocation is not so much to bind the religious who belong to the institute as to free them for the inspirations of the Spirit and needs of men. Their task is not to give detailed regulations for the daily life of various communities, but rather to provide a framework that brings balance and order into the life of the institute, from which peace will follow. And when there is peace, the community is wide open to the Spirit. In a way, we should say that the task of the general chapter is not to bind but to loose—not to bind by a great quantity of laws but to loose the ties that may be impediments to the free movement of the Spirit and to the service of our fellow men.

The right policy in legislation is to make a few laws only, formulated with clarity and simplicity. The temptation will arise to build up an elaborate legal system that would eliminate all loopholes and abuses, but this is not the purpose of our legislation, which should trust and serve the individuals and humbly accept the human fact that some evasions and abuses will always exist. When they arise we shall be humiliated and suffer from them; yet we should not penalize the whole community. Laws should not be conceived in terms of or in reference to the worst member of the community. Our limitations should be humbly accepted, and failures and abuses should be eliminated in some other way than by general legislation. The legal system itself should be flexible, open, trusting, and respectful of persons.

The members of the general chapter should keep in mind, also, that their task is to make general laws for the whole institute. They should leave plenty of room for differences in the provinces. Diversity comes from God just as much as unity: not to respect diversity is to flout the divine plan. Particular legislation could be provided by the provincial chapters, if particular laws are really needed.

The right hierarchy between laws, rules, and customs should be restored. These terms were frequently used as if they were synonymous. Constitutions, rule books, and custom books were promulgated by various organs of an institute, and then the same importance was attached to them, usually under the mistaken principle that a generous soul never distinguishes between great things and small: he wants to give all. It was concluded, accordingly, that there should be no difference in observance and in the machinery of dispensation. The fact is that God does distinguish between great things and small, and a generous soul must have the same mind that God has. He should distinguish between great commandments and small recommendations, and he should use his own judgment in adapting the written code to living persons and practical situations. Laws should be few and respected; no one wants anarchy. Rules should operate as guidelines, leaving a great amount of discretion to the individual so that he can follow the spirit rather than the letter of the rule. Customs should be what they are called: a common way of doing things. From this common way the person should be able to depart easily, whenever the circumstances postulate it— without any need for formal dispensation. Indeed, since customs are not rules, no one can dispense from them. This is not to suggest that some customs cannot become laws; it is simply an explanation of the role of customs. It would, however, be a rare case in modern times for a custom to become a law.

The legislative body of a religious community should keep in mind the great difference between the enclosed and the apostolic ways of life. In the enclosed way a great deal of uniformity is essential for the peace of the community; in the apostolic way such uniformity is harmful to the work. Therefore, the binding force of laws that do not deal with essential problems will be different in the two differing types of institute. The devotion of the enclosed religious is strongly centered on the holy rule. The devotion of those who follow the apostles' way of life should be strongly focused on the people of God who are entrusted to them. One of the primary needs of an enclosed religious is steadiness, stability; the primary need of an apostle is flexibility. The very character of laws, rules, and customs in an apostolic institute is different from that in an enclosed or monastic community. For the apostle working in the world, laws are instruments to help him to receive, to carry, and to announce God's message. That is one of the reasons why the legislation in an apostolic institute needs constant revision. Care should also be taken that laws should not accumulate; those that become antiquated should be canceled before they become an intolerable burden. Indeed, the principle of scholastic theologians is as valid today as it ever was: when a law is useless it is no longer law.

Finally, the subsidiary character of man-made laws should never be lost sight of. Priority over them should always be given to the authentic action of the Holy Spirit, and to the exigencies of the word of God. The children of God, particularly those especially consecrated to him, should feel and experience their freedom, as St. Paul experienced it. They should not be servants of the law; the law should be in their service. Part of the Good News is that God is interested in persons, not in observances. But full love will always be practical, doing the will of the Father as it is revealed through the Spirit, through the word, and through men sent by God.

THE EXERCISE OF EXECUTIVE POWER

When we speak about government in religious life we usually understand the exercise of executive power, but even short reflection makes it clear that the right government of an institute depends largely on the right function of legislative power. Superiors are really and only charged with the execution of the laws, with putting them into practice. As a rule no institute would give legislative power to superiors; it is always reserved for the chapters. The superior is usually entitled to interpret the laws for the sake of good government—in plainer language, he is entitled to make practical decisions without giving a final sentence about the meaning of the law. This is a wise rule, since life has to go on; someone has to cut short interminable discussions about the meaning of the law and call the community to action.

Good executive government exists when it is balanced between the legislator and those who hold some judicial power or authority to arbitrate. Hence the day-by-day government will be healthy if the superior faithfully follows the spirit and mind of the legislator, and is aware that he too can be called to account by another branch of authority in the institute. If the superior tries to invade the field of legislation, or if he becomes the sole arbiter of right and wrong, the right balance of the institute is upset and crisis will follow crisis. Every superior's first virtue, therefore, is obedience: he is bound by the constitutions. He should also have the humility to realize that he is helping with the dispensation of God's graces in a human situation where he does not have the gift of infallibility. He is permanently in need of help and correction.

Let us recall two principles that will help toward creating a balanced type of executive government. First, the gifts of God for the institute are given to the whole community—through every one who is a member of it. Second, there must be a source of unity, a unifying principle in every community. The first statement upholds diversity; the second one affirms the need for unity.

Diversity is necessary. Unless every member of the body functions fully and properly, the body cannot be healthy. The superior is bound in conscience to preserve diversity. Uniformity in itself has no religious value. The truth of this is so obvious that no further explanation is needed. This diversity should be present everywhere: in daily routine, in work, in relaxation, since in all these activities *different* persons are taking part.

Unity is necessary. The effort of the community has to be coordinated and guided, and this has to be done by authority. Otherwise there will be no community, but only a loose group exposed to dissolution at any time. This is a rule of common sense before being a rule of religious life. No business committee is allowed to function without a chairman. There is no state in which there is not *one* person who is finally entrusted with the execution of laws, be he called president or prime minister. In fact, no human community can exist if the final execution of the laws is entrusted to several persons: they would inevitably pull the community in different directions and would bring about its dissolution. The action of the community in a given case cannot be more than one; therefore, one mind must somehow lead it.

Although the community must have *one* head, the executive power itself can be variously distributed between the head and the members. To say that there must be one head does not mean that all the executive power must be with the head. In practice it is never so, but there are various ways of exercising power in government: one allows a large sharing of the power by the community, another concentrates most of the power in the hand of the superior. Both forms are good, both are confirmed by the experience of centuries. Their adoption in practice should depend on the traditions, purpose, and character of the institute. It would be quite wrong to pretend that there is a common solution for all. There is not. Communities are like human beings; each of them has its own personality. Moreover, while we are discussing these matters, let us recall that, however important the external structure of government is, the persons who are in charge are far more important.

In the one system (the more traditional one), the power to govern is shared by the community. Basic problems of policy and important administrative issues have to be brought before the brethren who have the right to decide by majority vote. The superior is bound by the decision, but he will remain fully in charge of its execution. There is, of course, both authority and obedience in this way of proceeding. Authority is exercised mainly in a corporate way, and all are bound to obey it. This type of government was familiar in monasteries, and a good deal of it was taken over by the friars of the Middle Ages. It is still practiced successfully in orders of ancient foundation. There are also some new institutes that are feeling their way in the same direction.

The key to the successful application of such a system is in an extremely rigorous selection of candidates and in maintaining the highest standards. Since decisions are taken by the majority, the spirit of the institute will in all ways reflect the view of the majority. The community will have an exceptional spirit if the majority is of exceptional quality; if they are not, the institute will sink into mediocrity. Accordingly, when a new foundation opts for this type of government, it should lay down exacting norms for admission, it should give an excellent training, and it should find some way to help back to secular life those who do not achieve the high standards.

In the other system (the more recent one), most of the power to govern is concentrated in one person, the superior. But then, since by necessity the superior represents the limited wisdom of *one* person, it will be necessary to establish a well-functioning machinery for steady consultation with the community and with various experts inside and even outside of the community so that the wisdom of one can be completed by the wisdom of many. There should also be an efficient machinery for correction if the decision was not the right one. The power to correct can be exercised in a binding way by a higher superior, or it can be exercised by way of advice through counselors.

In no circumstances should the consultations or corrections be reduced to mere formalities. Care should be taken also to choose the advisors or counselors of superiors in such a way that they represent different points of view. As a rule it would not be good policy to give the superior the right to appoint his own counsel. The temptation to choose persons who will easily agree with him is only too obvious. They could be elected by the community or appointed by a higher superior after consultation with the community.

The constitutions of religious institutes founded around or after the Council of Trent favor this type of government. If the superior is faithful to his duty of consultation and humble enough to take corrections, it can greatly increase speed in government and consequently apostolic efficiency. This system may also be helpful in giving scope to the best inspirations even if they come from a minority.

The person of the superior is of capital importance in this system. He must be well-versed in the art of discerning the will of God in this world, since his duty is not to create it but to find it. Moreover, he must be well trained in the human sciences that will help him in dealing with people. He should have qualities of leadership but abhor dictatorship.

Finally, it should be indicated that a combination of the two systems is possible—and actually exists in some communities. This happens when the whole community elects a group who will share the executive power of the superior, so that major issues would have to be decided by the vote of the majority in this elected group. The superior would remain in charge of execution. Such a group is sometimes called a *senate:* it helps the superior by sharing his power in a real way.

It may well be that such a solution will prove itself the best for many institutes. It does not give the power to govern to the majority, hence it helps to avoid a tendency to mediocrity. At the same time it sets up a structure to complete the wisdom of the superior, and to correct an imprudent course of action. There is a promising field here for experimentation.

A SEARCH FOR THE ESTABLISHMENT OF SOME JUDICIAL POWER IN RELIGIOUS INSTITUTES

The problem of judicial power in religious institutes remains a challenge. The problem can be stated with reasonable accuracy, but a good practical solution is not yet in

view. It is clear that some sort of judicial power is needed
in every community to keep the right balance between
general laws and their particular applications; between the
common good and personal rights. Further, it would be
desirable that doubts about the interpretation of the constitutions, the meaning of the rules, the observance of customs should be resolved by a panel of wise persons who are
not immediately involved in the administration, or in the
particular case. I am uncertain as to what the best practical
answer to this need is; I can only indicate some ideas that
may help us to find in due course the effective answer.

The judicial power or power of arbitration should not
be conceived exclusively as a legal institution to protect
the rights of the individual persons. It has to protect all
rights: those of the Church, of the institute, of the superior, and of the individual. It is in the interest of all that if
there is doubt about the law it should be resolved objec-
tively without any human respect. It is also for the good of
all that if there is an accusation of injustice against someone, a group not involved in the dispute should give a
considered and independent opinion. This would protect
the superior as much as the individual.

The institution of a tribunal with proper judicial
power is not alien to the law of the religious. Exempt
clerical orders have the right and duty to set up such a
tribunal in some cases of great importance, such as the
dismissal of one of their solemnly professed members.
Therefore, when we speak about judicial power we are
moving on solid and traditional ground.

The modern problem lies in determining how far to
extend the use of this power, its field of operation today. It
does not seem either necessary or wise to set up many judicial courts with jurisdiction. Rather we should think of

establishing a board of arbitrators composed of trusted, independent, and wise persons to whom cases of doubt and of apparent injustice could be referred. They could act on the petition according to their own discretion, and they could bring a judgment that would have an authority because of their integrity and prudence. It would not be necessary to confer jurisdiction on them. Such boards could be established within the framework of major institutes of men or women. They could function on provincial, regional, or universal levels depending on circumstances. For smaller institutes, perhaps, the diocese or the ecclesiastical province could establish such a board. Once the board is established, opportunity could be given to superiors and members in religious congregations to refer cases to it.

If the arbitrators are rightly selected, they could make a great contribution toward increasing respect for religious life. Through them it would be manifest to all inside and outside the Church that in our religious houses both the legitimate authority and the dignity of a Christian person are consistently upheld, and that, if an injustice occurs, it is neither covered up nor approved. Moreover, if the constitutions are finally interpreted by an independent tribunal, no arbitrary government could ever establish itself in a religious institute. To avoid such governments forever in the future would greatly serve the cause of the Church and the greater glory of God.

CONCLUSION

The changing of some structures in government in no way destroys authority. The power given by the Church to a religious institute is there whether the government is exer-

cised in a more corporate or a more personal way. Obedience in all cases is exactly the same: the emptying of a
person to the will of God. In fact, this chapter has been
precisely a search: how can a religious institute and those
in government best empty themselves to receive the will
of God.

In this search the intention has been, not so much to
offer ready-made solutions, as to present some ideas that
may serve as a point of departure for further reflection and
perhaps for eventual experimentation. The gifts of the
Spirit and of nature are given to each of us, and, with their
help, we should go on searching. Each institute should
build up the type of government that best suits its traditions and its vocation in the future. To find the right type
of government is to set out on the road to progress. Good
administration and good persons in office will open up the
institute to the Holy Spirit, will help the members to follow Christ closely, and will make them servants of their
fellow man.

As long as we do not have good practical solutions let
us go on searching. In this way we can initiate and keep up
that perpetual work of renewal that the Council asks from
us and which may well be the ordinary way of life of religious in the future. In fact, this perpetual search and im-
provement is the only way to keep us open to the Holy
Spirit and to the needs of this world that God loved so
much that he gave his only Son for its redemption.

7

Filled with Grace and Power:
Contemplation

A first reading of the Decree *Perfectae Caritatis* may give the impression that the document is no more than a codification of the spirit and the structure of religious life as it existed at the time of Vatican Council II. But a closer study of the text reveals deep insights that lead to unexpected developments in religious life. A sentence that contains a new vision and is likely to have a great impact in the future, is: "To this end, as they seek God before all things and only Him, the members of each community should combine contemplation with apostolic love" (Abbott, p. 470).

The Council statement is firm and clear: all religious are called to both contemplation and apostolic love; therefore, there cannot be any distinction between so-called contemplative and apostolic institutes. If such a distinction existed in the past, it should not continue. Since all institutes, without exception, have to be contemplative and apostolic at the same time, these two characters should be present in their spirit and their external structure. If some distinctions are still necessary, they can apply only to different types of contemplation and different types of apostolic action. It follows that in all institutes there is a common element of contemplation that can be determined and described; otherwise, all of them could not be contemplative. Similarly, in all institutes there is a *common* element of apostolic action; otherwise, not all could be apostolic. There is, however, a variation in putting into practice these contemplative and apostolic aspects. This chapter will concentrate on explaining the contemplative side, or the contemplative depth of consecrated life. The following one will deal with the apostolic aspects.

THE UNITY BETWEEN CONTEMPLATION AND APOSTOLIC ACTION

To understand unity in the life of a community, the best approach is to consider unity in the life of an individual. The unity of the individual's life will be reflected in the life of the community.

Every human being has a reflective mind and will power. Notionally we can distinguish the acts of the mind and the acts of the will, but both the vision of the mind and the pursuits of the will have their roots in the whole person. Although they are different signs of life, therefore analytically distinguishable, they are one in their source. They are one because the person himself is one.

When the members are united in community life, we find the manifestations of reflective minds—insights and intuitions. We find, as well, signs of will power—creative acts and practical love. All of them, theoretical insights and practical actions, have their roots in the one and undivided community. At their source, vision and love cannot

be separated. Similarly, in the life of a religious community, the contemplation of God's mighty deeds and the
building of his kingdom cannot be separated. They spring
from one source; they are two aspects of the same life, the
life of the community.

Yet, because we do not have a comprehensive intuition of the whole reality, either of a human person or of a
community, we distinguish the two aspects and speak first
of contemplation and then of apostolic action. But it
should be made clear that the distinction is mainly con-
ceptual. It divides equitably what is a vital unity. Such
division is, of course, possible in the realm of ideas, but not
in the real world. If that happened, it would result in
tragedy. A person who has creative insights, but does not
follow them up by actions, achieves nothing. A person who
has a strong will but no insight is a source of danger for
himself and for his community. The contemplative and
apostolic aspects of religious life are therefore the twofold
signs of one life that cannot be divided without destroying
that life itself. The division exists only in our mind, and
the work of analysis is no more than a useful procedure to
understand the depth and the riches of a person or community.

CONTEMPLATION: A PRELIMINARY DEFINITION

Contemplation is a rich term. It has defied theological definition for centuries—and no wonder, for contemplation
is a vital gift from God, and God's gifts rarely tolerate the
narrow limits of our concepts. Nevertheless, we cannot
leave contemplation, fully clouded in mystery. To discuss
our topic, we need some description, and the Council

comes to our help with a short and excellent phrase: "[By contemplation] they adhere to God in mind and heart" (Abbott, *loc. cit.*).

Two elements immediately emerge from this definition. First, contemplation means to adhere to the divine Persons; second, it means to adhere to God in both mind *and* heart. *To adhere* is the literal translation of the Latin word "adhaerere," whose root meaning (as it is in English, too) is to cling to someone, to be attached to someone, or, in a stronger form, to live and to move with someone. Contemplation, therefore, means the adhesion of a human person to the divine Persons; a direct, personal relationship between God and man, without the mediation of created things or concepts. This relationship has to exist between God and every member of the community, and, through the persons, between God and the whole community; individual persons and the whole community have to adhere to God.

Such a communication with God involves the whole human person: man has to cling to God with mind and heart. *To adhere in mind* implies somehow the obscure vision of God through faith; *to adhere in heart* implies firm love of God. No man can adhere to another person without knowing the other. No man can adhere to God in his mind without having some experiential knowledge of God through those inspirations and promptings of the Holy Spirit about which St. Paul wrote so many times. Progress in Christian maturity means (among other developments) progress in this experience of God's presence.

This personal relationship implies also a "clinging" to God with our heart. In ordinary terms this means to love God, with a love that transcends any affection for created persons and things, and terminates in the divine Persons.

Some of this intuitive love is necessary for all Christians. To grow *in* Christ means to grow in this love.

The Council description of contemplation is impregnated with rich meaning. It brings out the personal element in our relationship with God, and the commitment of the whole person of God. This definition will have great importance for our future investigation. It should be understood from now on that a contemplative person (and all religious are called to be that) *cannot* find God either in other human persons or in created things unless he has found God first, personally, by adhering to God in his own mind and heart. Nothing less than personal friendship with God can fully satisfy a human person.

THEOLOGICAL FOUNDATION OF THE COUNCIL'S DEFINITION

The Council's definition of contemplation is the fruit of the understanding of the working of theological virtues in a Christian person. To adhere to God with mind and heart means to live the life of faith, hope, and charity. These three virtues are like three rivers springing from the same source—sanctifying grace, the baptismal grace. This grace is the effect of God's glorious and powerful presence in a Christian, so that ultimately contemplation is the fruit of the presence of the Spirit, a fruit produced through the virtues of faith, hope, and charity. Let us consider how faith, hope, and charity lead to this adhering to God.

The virtue of faith usually implies both the subjective capacity to see the mystery revealed by God through his Son and the acceptance of God's objective message that comes to us in human words. Although faith is a free act in man, it is principally a virtue of the intellect. It lifts up a human being by giving him the power to see God and the created world in the same way as God sees them. This does not mean that the Christian will have the same depth of vision that God has; but it does mean that in some points his vision will coincide with God's. This coincidence may indeed be restricted; yet, it exists. In the truth of the statement *the Word was made flesh* the mind of God and man meet. Both are in possession of the same truth, although the depth of divine knowledge is at an infinite distance from the shallowness of our knowledge. Nevertheless, the two minds coincide; they are united in the *one* truth. To adhere to God in faith means to adapt our mind to God's; St. Paul calls this the obedience of faith. To develop in this union with God means to extend our vision of faith more and more. To adhere to God is therefore a dynamic concept; it involves continuous progress in this intuitive knowledge of faith. The coincidence between God's and man's vision should grow until the human mind is fully submitted to, and directed by, the mind of God.

To possess the virtue of hope means to rely on the fidelity of God on our way to his kingdom. To hope is to anticipate the reality of the kingdom and of all the spiritual and material means necessary for reaching the kingdom. To hope in God means to seek our own fulfillment in the gifts God offers us. The best of these gifts is God himself and his blessed life that we will share; other gifts are all the created persons and things that can help us on our way to God. To adhere to God in hope means to be in possession of a security that comes from the word of God and from the presence of the Holy Spirit in us. The presence of the Spirit gives assurance *now* of the *future* revelation of the glory of the children of God; of the glory that is actually already ours.

The more our heart is open to the possession of God,

the more he leads us back to the world to find his image written into everything. The virtue of hope means to adhere to God who is in this world and beyond this world, to God who gives us this world and the one to come. To grow in the virtue of hope means to possess God more strongly and to possess the world in God more firmly.

To have the theological virtue of charity is the highest participation in God's life. It is to have a share in the divine abundance and in the divine act of giving. When the goodness and humanity of God is apprehended by a man, and when he is attracted by God's infinite beauty so much that he wants to give all that he has to God his Father and to the other children of God, then he is acting under the impulse of divine charity. For a Christian, God and man are not two distinct objects of charity. He loves God and he loves God's image in man. His generous act of giving with God in sight extends to God's whole family: to those sanctified by the Spirit and to those waiting for their redemption. Progress in charity means an increase in the intensity of this attitude of giving. To adhere to God in charity means that there is no pause in the desire to give and in the practical acts of giving. Charity cannot stand still; it is a dynamic virtue. To adhere to God in charity is to share God's dynamic love for himself and for all men.

To adhere to God in mind and in heart means to adhere to God in faith, hope, and charity. The theological virtues are the source and the realization of the contemplation about which the Council speaks. They are three, the three fruits or three manifestations of *one* reality. The one reality is the person of a child of God who received the wisdom and the power of the Spirit and therefore has a new capacity to see and a new capacity to love. Finally, the source of this unique grace is the living Spirit of God in him: sanctifying grace is nothing less than the transformation of a human person into a child of God because of the presence of the Spirit in him. Without this presence, grace and virtues would be meaningless. They are the effects of the living presence of the Spirit, as light and warmth are the effects of the presence of fire. Here we reach the final source of contemplation, the Holy Spirit—it is he who teaches us to pray by crying out "Abba, Father," and teaches us to love through making us the servant of God and of our fellow men. *He adheres to us,* so that we can adhere to him.

Through consideration of the theological virtues, the strongly personal character of our relationship with God emerges again with a new clarity. Through the theological virtues, we are united to him; through the growth of the same virtues, our union with him increases. To understand more about the contemplative aspects of religious life, we have to inquire into the meaning of our union with God.

SOME FALSE MEANINGS OF UNION WITH GOD

If contemplation means to adhere to *God,* there is contemplation as far as there is union with him, and whenever there is union with him, there is contemplation. But the terms should not be understood in a static way, for both contemplation and union are dynamic. They cannot exist in a permanently unchangeable state because life means movement—either forward or backward, but movement. Where there is no movement there is no life.

The expression "union with God" is frequently used in spiritual books and conferences. It is presented as the aim and purpose of our religious life, as the goal of our spiritual pilgrimage. But this union is rarely described or explained, which is surprising since it has to take the central place in our whole life. The search for the meaning of contemplation has led us to the problem of union with God; hence, to understand contemplation, the meaning of union has to be clarified. We are in a delicate and sensitive area where the opinions of various schools clash, and the lack of a commonly accepted terminology clouds the issue. Methodologically, the best approach to the problem seems to be to consider first the case of a fully matured union with God, and afterwards its initial and progressive development towards maturity. Such a method is based on common sense. No one can know what the seed contains unless he knows the tree that grows out of the seed. By the same principle it is clear that we cannot hope to know what this union with God is, unless we know it in its maturity. But before describing the positive content of this union, the ground should be cleared by discarding some concepts that cannot be accepted. Once this is done, the positive doctrine, construed on clear ground, can have its effect.

Two extreme explanations of union with God have to be rejected. Such union is not identical with perfect legal observances, and it does not consist in an extraordinary experience of God's presence. The legal approach has a sound starting point, for it describes the maturity of our union with God as the perfect fulfillment of God's will. Then, however, a shift in the emphasis develops, and God's will is fully identified with the observance of laws, rules, customs, commands, and precepts. It is stated that all that is required in order to achieve union with God is to observe perfectly these norms or orders. The scrupulous and meticulous execution of these external promptings would be synonymous with union with God. We should willingly admit that the will of God can be revealed through the "ministry" of laws, and that legitimate authorities in the Church have power "to bind and to loose," but we should never think that Christian maturity, or close union with God, can ever be achieved by, or ever consist in, sheer legal observances. Prudent fidelity to laws can be a help towards union; wise external forms can construct a framework in which the union operates, but they cannot be the union. The personal knowledge and love of God is not identical with external norms and forms. Man's heart cannot be satisfied with them; every man wants a living person for friend. Laws and observances have meaning only insofar as they carry a personal message between friends, and as they lead to a person; otherwise, they are empty and can be an actual hindrance in finding the desired person. Above all, God is delighted by being with a human person; the Scriptures never tell us that he finds pleasure in discipline for discipline's sake. It follows that however perfect the observance of external norms may be, it cannot effect union with God. In saying this, I am simply repeating the doctrine of St. Paul that the law cannot bring life because life comes from God.

Another opinion goes to the opposite extreme. It describes the maturity of our union with God as an ecstatic experience of God's presence, even to a degree that transcends the common Christian experience recorded in the New Testament. Some texts in the writings of St. John of the Cross can be construed as supporting this view. At a more ordinary level, spiritual writers who insist that Christians progressing in virtue should reach a state where they are granted dramatic and extraordinary experiences of God implicitly profess the same doctrine, although they may not be aware of the full implications of their words. We often find similar suggestions in the biographies of saintly persons. Their unusual experiences are presented as signs of maturity or maturity itself—called more than once the "state of perfection." Their miraculous deeds, or the ecstatic spiritual communications they receive from God, are identified with sanctity and union with God. More implicitly than explicitly, it is conveyed to the reader that the extraordinary events and experiences represent the fullness of Christian maturity. It is not difficult to see how misleading such doctrine is. The argument against it is simple: no theory or reasoning is valid if it is contradicted by facts, and a clear fact in the life of the Church is that many persons achieved Christian maturity without such extraordinary experiences. Some obvious examples are St. Thomas More, St. Peter Canisius, St. Robert Bellarmine. They adhered to God in mind and heart, in life and death, and yet their spiritual life was simplicity itself. Their experiences could have been described in common biblical terms.

It is obviously not my intention to deny that events out of the ordinary may occur in the life of saints, or even in the life of sinners; neither would I contest that some persons may receive the gift of perceiving the presence of God in themselves, and that such perception can reach extraordinary heights or depths—as it did in the case of St. Paul, of St. Teresa, or of St. Ignatius of Loyola. Yet neither the prodigies, nor the most sublime communications from God can constitute the essence of union, in other words, full Christian maturity. The reason for this view is primarily empirical: many are they who reached maturity, but did not go through extraordinary experiences. The best confirmation comes from a legion of martyrs, especially in modern times, who could not have had a greater love because they laid down their life for Christ, and yet they did not give any sign of having received ecstatic communications from God. There is, moreover, a doctrinal reason for the view here set forth. The indwelling of the Holy Spirit is the greatest gift a man can receive. Any experience in human consciousness is of lesser importance, even if it is the fruit of the presence of the Spirit. The existing reality is the presence of God; an extraordinary experience of it is a transient event. But Christian maturity cannot consist in a transient event; it must be in a permanent reality.

Let us conclude, therefore, that union with God is no more rooted in ecstatic experiences than it is in legal observances. There remains the question: what then is this union with God?

BIBLICAL BACKGROUND: THE TEXT FROM MATTHEW

The problem cannot be adequately treated unless we go back to the Bible for inspiration. It would be more than helpful to search all the books of the Old and the New Covenant for the meaning of union with God, but this is impossible within our limited scope. Much inspiration can nevertheless be found in some prominent biblical themes.

The text most frequently quoted in reference to our union with God is in the Gospel of St. Matthew: "You must therefore be perfect just as your heavenly Father is perfect" (Mt 5, 48). The exegesis of this text is complex and it cannot be done without reference to the Old Testament and to the preceding verses in chapter five of Matthew. There is a parallel text in the Old Testament: "Be holy, for I, Yahweh your God, am holy" (Lev 19, 2). For

the Israelite of the Old Covenant, holiness meant, not
so much a moral perfection as the presence of God's
glory or power in a place or person. This sense is very
strong all through the Old Testament, and it is preserved
in St. Paul's writings. Matthew's Gospel reflects the
Hebrew mind, and therefore this mysterious "perfection,"
which is equivalent to holiness, must be also a gift from
God: God's glory and power present in a man. Indeed,
in a Hebrew context, any idea of perfection by way
of moral achievement, or by way of an immutable state,
should be excluded, for it cannot adequately render
the thought of the Evangelist. Moreover, the word
perfect is not a good translation of the corresponding
original Greek term in Matthew's text, although it
would be difficult, if not impossible, to conceive a better
translation. We are dealing with one of those cases where
the two languages do not communicate for lack of common
expressions. The Greek term in Matthew is *teleioi,* in reference to the disciples; and *teleios,* in reference to God.
Now, *telos* in Greek means aim, end, goal, purpose—which
is not exactly the same as perfection. The best approxima-
tion to the meaning of the Greek would be: fulfill the
purpose of your existence, as your heavenly Father fulfills
it. This is not a very meaningful sentence; but it contains
elements missed by the common translation. The preceding verses in Matthew speak of love: Christ enjoins his
disciples to have a universal love for all men, for friends
and for enemies.

> You have learnt how it was said: You must love your
> neighbour and hate your enemy. But I say this to you:
> Love your enemies and pray for those who persecute
> you; in this way you will be sons of your Father in
> heaven, for he causes his sun to rise on bad men as well

as good, and his rain to fall on honest and dishonest men alike. For if you love those who love you, what right have you to claim any credit? Even the tax collectors do as much, do they not? And if you save your greetings for your brothers, are you doing anything exceptional? Even the pagans do as much, do they not? You must therefore be perfect just as your heavenly Father is perfect (Mt 5, 43–48).

Jesus really is revealing the overwhelming abundance of God's love that extends to all men, and he enjoins his disciples to have the same love. Matthew concludes the reporting of Jesus' command by the *logion,* saying, of Jesus: the disciples should fulfill the purpose of their existence as the heavenly Father fulfills it. This purpose is to love. The disciples should have the same indiscriminating, overwhelming abundance of love for every human person as the heavenly Father has. This love, of course, like holiness, is a power infused into the heart of man by God; no one can give it to himself. It is clear, now, why the original text is not well rendered by the modern word perfect. Matthew's thought loses much of its richness, and suffers a shift in emphasis when it is translated into modern English. Christ does not call his disciples to some sort of abstract moral perfection; he calls them to accept the gift of this wholesome love from his Father. The preceding sayings of Jesus make it clear also that this love has to be practical. A fair explanation, if not a translation of verse 48 could be: Love all men in deeds, as your heavenly Father loves them in deeds; or: have the same universal and practical love in yourself that your heavenly Father has in himself. However we may try, the translation will remain poor, because there is no perfect correspondence between Greek and English in this case. But our efforts were not in vain: it is certain that the saying of Jesus, as it is recorded by St. Matthew, does not support a conception of union with God which would consist in an abstract perfection—so familiar in the writings of many Greek philosophers. The positive elements that emerge from the text and context are the praise of Jesus for universal and practical charity as the distinguishing mark of his disciples, and the conception that such a love is the power and glory of God present in a mortal man. The parallel text of Luke fully confirms this interpretation. It reads: "Be compassionate as your Father is compassionate" (Lk 6, 36).

BIBLICAL BACKGROUND: THE KINGDOM AND THE SPIRIT

The maturity of our union with God cannot be anything else than the maturity of the kingdom of God within us. Some examples will show what Jesus taught about his kingdom, and how he explained its development to his disciples. He liked to use parables that implied the presence of the kingdom both on earth and in the heart of the disciples and its dynamic character. "The kingdom of heaven," he said, "is like a mustard seed" (Mt 13, 31). There is a hidden strength in the seed: once it falls into the soil, it will develop into a tree. The parable describes a dynamic reality. Christ also compared the kingdom with the yeast that a woman mixed with flour until it was leavened all through (Mt 13, 33). Christ did not impress on us the image of a "perfect" static state that would correspond to the kingdom. He spoke only of an ever-increasing and developing life. The kingdom is life, filled with dynamic strength; the kingdom in us is an unceasing movement toward God. Our union with God has the same qualities. It develops as the seed develops into a tree. It is a process of transformation, as the action of the yeast on the flour is a dynamic process of transformation.

The union with God, then, is life and movement. The practical conclusion is that we should not seek any state, but should join in a movement. But what exactly is this movement—where is its origin and where does it lead?

We find an answer to these questions in the writings of St. Paul. His was a dynamic personality that helped him to understand the living strength present in God's kingdom. Further, he was an apostle with the mind of a theologian. He not only preached the good news, but he also explained the divine forces operating in Christ's new creation.

Paul preached incessantly that we are children of God; the proof of our adoption is the presence of the Spirit in our hearts:

> The proof that you are sons is that God has sent the Spirit of his Son into our hearts: the Spirit that cries, "Abba, Father" and it is this that makes you a son, you are not a slave any more; and if God has made you son, then he has made you heir (Gal 4, 6–7).

This union with the Spirit fulfills the purpose of our creation. This is a major theme in Paul's gospel, meant for all Christians, including persons consecrated to God. God's purpose in giving us life and redemption was to give us the life in the Spirit: "This is the purpose for which God made us, and he has given us the pledge of the Spirit" (2 Cor 5, 5).

It is good to pause and reflect here for a moment: God's purpose in giving us existence and grace was not to have a people who would serve him with perfect legal observances; it was not to have persons who would seek ecstatic experiences in mind, heart, and soul, but it was to have children who could take part in the life of the divine Persons in an intelligent, loving, and free way. He "installs" us in this new vocation by "marking us with his seal and giving us the pledge, the Spirit, that we carry in our hearts" (2 Cor 1, 22).

Nothing is further from the mind of Paul than an impersonal religion, or a religion that would connect us with God through created persons or things. There has to be a personal relationship between God's child and God's Spirit. This relationship is a living one, it is full of action, personal exchanges, communications of knowledge and of love. Through this relationship with the Spirit we become coheirs of Christ:

> In fact, unless you possessed the Spirit of Christ you would not belong to him . . . The spirit you received is not the spirit of slaves bringing fear into your lives again; . . . And if we are the children we are heirs as well: heirs of God and coheirs with Christ, sharing his sufferings so as to share his glory (Rom 8, 9, 14, 17).

The same Spirit of God who effects our incorporation into Christ brings us to our Father, not as slaves or conquered enemies, but as free children of God:

> The spirit you received is not the spirit of slaves bringing fear into your lives again; it is the spirit of sons, and it makes us cry out, "Abba, Father!" (Rom 8, 15).

Union with God for Paul means to pray, to move and live with the divine Persons. This union includes a steady progress in understanding:

> Now instead of the spirit of the world, we have received the Spirit that comes from God, to teach us to understand the gifts that he has given us (1 Cor 2, 12).

This new knowledge comes from the Spirit who reaches the depth of God and man:

> These are the very things that God has revealed to us through the Spirit, for the Spirit reaches the depths of everything, even the depths of God (1 Cor 2, 10).

No more intimate communication between God and man is possible. With the knowledge of God love is given:

> . . . and this hope is not deceptive, because the love of God has been poured into our hearts by the Holy Spirit which has been given us (Rom 5, 5).

The love of God is universal and knows no limits. It is also practical. Paul describes it with an abundance of terms:

> What the Spirit brings is very different: love, joy, peace, patience, kindness, goodness, trustfulness, gentleness, and self-control (Gal 5, 22).

He leaves no doubt that the practical love of our fellow men is the sign of the love infused into our heart by the Spirit. To have the Spirit is to share the universal love of God who

> causes his sun to rise on bad men as well as good and his rain to fall on honest and dishonest men alike (Mt 5, 45).

The well known text from the first Epistle to the Corinthians sums up Paul's gospel:

> Be ambitious for the higher gifts. And I am going to show you a way that is better than any of them. If I have all the eloquence of men or of angels, but speak without love I am simply a gong booming or a cymbal clashing . . . In short, there are three things that last: faith, hope and love; and the greatest of these is love (1 Cor 12, 31; 13, 1; 13, 13).

Even from such a short study of the writings of St. Paul, it is clear that union with God means a dynamic union with the Holy Spirit who then introduces the new-born man into personal relationship with the divine Persons—without any created intermediary. Paul's religious conception is intensely personal, it is based on personal communication with God. But such an intense sharing of God's life does not turn man's attention away from the world; on the contrary, it makes him more aware of the need for a new birth for the whole creation:

> . . . but creation still retains the hope of being freed, like us, from its slavery to decadence, to enjoy the same freedom and glory as the children of God (Rom 8, 21).

The love that the Spirit gives is so abundant that it cannot exist without being poured out into the world, hence the children of God show practical charity that impregnates the smallest details of their daily life as certainly as the sun gives light and warmth.

For St. Paul such a union with God brings with it the experience of God—but not in an ecstatic way: Paul wrote his letters to ordinary Christians. The experience is not centered on great transient spiritual events, but on the quiet realizations that God is a living person in living contact with man. Paul himself carefully distinguishes his "visions and revelations" and his being caught up "into the third heaven" from his steady reliance on the Spirit, from his devotion to Jesus who is the Lord, and from his prayer to the Father.

Union with God is also a dynamic process that has no end or final term to it in this world. The pilgrim's progress will be consummated in the eternal kingdom of God when all will be one in Christ, and Christ will offer the whole creation to his Father. The source of this unity is the action of the Spirit.

SOME PRACTICAL CONSIDERATIONS

From the reading of the biblical texts it is clear that the source of faith, hope, and charity is the Holy Spirit present in a child of God. Therefore, the aim and purpose of every Christian should be to live with the Spirit of God. In other words, the more a Christian lives under the impact of the Holy Spirit, the more he is united to God. In the life of each one of us, there is a field which is dominated by the Holy Spirit, a field where we move with faith, hope, and love. There is a field also which escapes this influence of the Spirit and where we are led by our own selfishness. The more extended the field in which the Spirit moves us, the more united we are to God.

This union cannot be fully described in general terms because it is so intensely personal. Nor can its stages of development be defined adequately. Every friendship, even among humans, is unique and does not conform to a precise pattern. When one of the friends is God himself, then the unique character of the friendship becomes even more striking. Since God is the leading partner, the aim of man should be to follow God's inspirations. Man's principal intention should not be to achieve a certain "state," or "to perfect himself morally"; it should be to live, to move with another person.

A practical consequence immediately emerges. Great care should be taken that those who are taking their first steps in the spiritual life, whether they are novices in a religious institute or not, should not be misled by an abstract image of perfection; their vision and their inclinations should be directed towards a living Person. To impress on them that they are called to be "perfect" can be misleading; it can convey the idea that Christian maturity consists in an immutable happy state, not clouded by the shadows of this world. There is not a shred of evidence in the Scriptures to substantiate such a doctrine; our Lord himself was deeply disturbed on the eve of his passion and death. Beginners should be taught rather to adhere to God in mind and heart; they should be taught to converse with a living Person. In other words, their minds and hearts should not be directed to a distant ideal to be eventually achieved, but to a Person present and talking to them here and now.

This doctrine can have a liberating effect on religious persons and their communities. It excludes tension that results from the contemplation of an ideal "state" in the future as compared to present realities. Many religious have a mental image of their "perfect" self and are aware, at the same time, of their "imperfections." The result is a tension that takes its toll on their internal and external life. More than once, even after many years in religion, the tension results in a sense of failure when the person realizes that the chances to transform himself to the abstract image are small or, more realistically, nil. If such a stage is reached, he may remain within the cloister, and even be observant, but he will not be happy or generous.

A similar psychological block may be created in a community. Each has its ideal of perfection—it is described in the constitutions; but each community also realizes its own shortcomings. In order to bridge the gap between the ideal and the reality, the community may assume unnecessary rules and observances, which do not make it any holier but will cover the gap. As in the case of the individual, so in the life of the community, strains and tensions are bound to develop, and general unhappiness can become the order of the day, accepted usually as the inevitable consequence of their consecration to God. Nothing is farther from the truth.

If both persons and communities concentrate on being faithful to a Person, the situation changes. There is no need to contemplate a distant ideal, there is every need to concentrate on the wishes of a Person here and now. The measure of progress is not in the conformity to a distant image, but in the prompt response to a living Person. Moreover, if one does not respond, there is no irreversible failure, since the Person does not cease talking to us in many ways. The conversation, if interrupted by lack of attention or unfaithfulness, can be resumed again without delay.

We do not know where such a "clinging to God in mind and heart" will lead: it is an adherence in faith. Each person will develop in a different way, and in each the progress will be in right proportion with the increase of his faith, hope, and charity. Each community will fulfill an historical role in the life of the Church, if it remains open all the time to the new inspirations of the Spirit. Failures and shortcomings should not unduly upset any community: they have their place in God's plan.

It is wrong to assume that God effectively wants every person in religion to reach a "state of perfection." True, with some he wants to achieve great purity of heart here on earth, but for others he reserves this gift for the moment when they enter eternity. God wants fidelity from all, but he builds his kingdom in the hearts of man step by step.

This realistic conception of our union with God can further transform the life of religious communities. If all are centered on a Person and not on an ideal, there will be less worry about "perfection," but more care about helping each other. The apostolic command to carry each other's burden will become a reality. If God wants fidelity from all, but does not effectively desire all to reach a perfect state, the members should have great understanding of and patience toward each other. They should realize that God's time has not yet come for "perfect" virtue. A very imperfect person can be a faithful disciple.

There will be no need for a subtle mask to hide faults and give the impression of non-existing virtues. If it is taken for granted that the community is a gathering of those who are in need of being healed from their infirmities, no one will be surprised if he sees the weakness of others. And he will not be tempted to hide his own weakness with a superhuman effort that paralyzes his progress.

An atmosphere of sincerity can reign in communities where all are convinced that their vocation is to adhere to God in mind and heart. Sincerity brings peace and releases energy for constructive work. The attitude of the members toward each other will not be that of criticism or the desire to correct, but an attitude of encouragement to fidelity to the Spirit. Is there not more Christian humility in this way of life than in many artifical exercises?

In this climate of openness formalities are excluded from the life of the community as a foreign body, since every formality is a distortion of reality. Formality, here, means, not simply an external form (it may be necessary), but an external form without content. An empty formality is a practical lie, a distortion of God's beautiful world.

The necessary external forms take their place naturally. They are needed; they follow and they witness our humanity that God himself wanted to share, but these laws will not kill the spirit; they will rather free the person for receiving the Spirit—as all Christian laws and religious rules should.

A religious community united to God in this way is certainly a sign of the kingdom. It is far more—it is the fire that Christ brought upon the earth.

We have steered our way between two somewhat extreme and opposite doctrines to a balanced theory which is inspired by the Scripture, is in harmony with our tradition, and confirmed by sound practical sense. This approach can be the source of deep peace in religious life, and even if one fails from time to time, the remedy will be obvious: to return to the Person, to follow his promptings by accepting his inspirations and by doing his will. To this union, all religious are called.

THE EXPERIENCE OF GOD'S PRESENCE

From the concept of union let us return to that of contemplation. Union is a fact, contemplation is action. Union could, perhaps, exist without any perception of it, but contemplation necessarily implies some knowledge of it, because no one can adhere to God in mind and heart without having some certainty in mind and heart that he is clinging to God. What is the nature of this perception? How far does Christian maturity, or indeed, progress toward this maturity, include the experience of union? An answer has been given by St. Paul: in the consciousness of a Christian there is an experience of the prompting of the Spirit who leads us to Christ and to the Father. But can this experience be described with more precision or clarity?

Let us not forget that this experience is, of its very nature, obscure. Any description of it will necessarily be inadequate; but an attempt can be made to throw more light on the issue.

A fundamental statement opens the way for further

consideration: a Christian is aware of the gift of grace, or, in more technical terms, a Christian is able to know if he is in the state of grace. Unfortunately, there is a lot of confusion on this point. St. Paul would no doubt have been astonished and provoked to a vehement reaction if anyone had told him that a Christian could not know if he has the Spirit or not. The whole teaching of Paul proves the opposite. Many spiritual books nevertheless propose the doctrine that no one can know if he is in the state of grace, and then they capitalize on this presumed uncertainty to induce the reader to practice humility. They usually rely on the Council of Trent, where it is stated that no one can have an absolute and infallible certitude (unless he receives a special revelation) that he will persevere to the end of his life in the service of God. But the doctrine of Trent was an answer to the Reformers, some of whom asserted that man can have such knowledge, and it is not a correction of Paul's or John's teaching, or of the whole New Testament. Christians can be aware of the presence of the Spirit, and consequently of the gift of grace. This awareness is not an infallible divine certainty, but a quiet security granted by God present. It is not a clear intellectual apprehension; it is an intuition of God's children. It manifests itself in peace, joy, and contentment in the service of God, or better, in faith, hope, and charity. It is expressed by a good conscience. This awareness of grace is necessary: unless someone is convinced that he is loved by God, he will never respond to that love. If someone does not know, or even cannot know with certainty that God loves him, he cannot give himself and all his possessions to God. It would be against the most elementary law of human nature.

A Christian is a person to whom it is given to be

aware of the Spirit and of the gifts of the Spirit. Without this fundamental statement any discourse about contemplation would be meaningless. Contemplation is really the experience of the Spirit and his gifts—sometimes with great intensity.

But Christian awareness of the presence of the Spirit and his gifts is not to be confused with an ecstatic state. It is still less the immediate vision of God, the vision of God which will be given us only in heaven. There is now an incapacity in us to see God face to face, an incapacity so radical that God will have to give us a new gift to enter into his glory. Theologians describe this gift by the expression light of glory, *lumen gloriae*. Without it, the beatific vision is not possible. The common Christian experience here on earth is not the beatific vision nor the full vision of the grace of God within us.

Christian experience includes, however, the quiet enjoyment, and also the reflexive knowledge of the fruits of God's presence. They penetrate into our conscious self. The Holy Spirit gives new eyes to those who receive the faith to see God's mysterious work. It is enough to read the account of any convert from the time of the apostles to this day. They all speak about a new vision that brought them contentment and happiness. This change is the effect of God's invisible action on their conscious mind. Further, the presence of the Holy Spirit can give security to a person through the infusion of the virtue of hope. This security would be meaningless unless it is experienced. Finally, it is enough to read Christian literature, and to see how an act of giving in the name of Christ brings joy and happiness to the heart. The new vision, the security, the joy in giving are the perception, the effect in the conscious mind of a hidden force that comes from God. Union with

God means an experience. It does not mean the immediate vision of God or the direct perception of God's grace. It means the enjoyment of God's power, strength, and glory that penetrates, in an obscure way, into the consciousness of a child of God. It transforms his mind, it transforms his heart, gives him new insights, new attractions and new satisfactions.

Theologians can, of course, reflect on the fact of this obscure experience. They can point out that it is like looking at the fruit of a plant whose roots we cannot see because they are deep down in the ground. Or, using a different analogy, they may say that we are like blind persons who feel the warmth of the sun but cannot see its light. Such comparisons, imperfect as they are, help us to realize and understand that the experience of the Spirit exists and is an integral part of our Christian life. The very acceptance of a call from God to religious life implies this experience, although the person who receives the call may not be able to explain what is happening in him.

The development of a religious vocation depends a great deal on the development of this experience because, the more sensitive a person or a community is to the promptings of the Holy Spirit, the closer their union with God will be. Therefore, the life of a person as well as the life of a community should be organized in such a way that this experience can be protected and helped. Freedom from worries and opportunities for silent prayer will be the best means to foster it. The experience, however, will display the same varieties as the union itself. It is the experience of a friendship, and since every friendship is unique, its experience will also be unique. Sometimes it will consist in a simple contentment in doing the will of God; sometimes, it will be mute suffering in accepting that will. But in both cases it will be an authentic experience of God's presence.

All Christians are consecrated to God through their baptism; those who undertake the life of the evangelical counsels are dedicated to God under a new and special title. The Council explains this in its Dogmatic Constitution on the Church:

> [A religious] is totally dedicated to God by an act of supreme love, and is committed to the honor and service of God under a new and special title.
>
> It is true that through baptism he has died to sin and has been consecrated to God. However, in order to derive more abundant fruit from this baptismal grace, he intends, by the profession of the evangelical counsels in the Church, to free himself from those obstacles which might draw him away from the fervor of charity and the perfection of divine worship. Thus he is more intimately consecrated to divine service. This consecration gains in perfection since by virtue of firmer and steadier bonds it serves as a better symbol of the unbreakable link between Christ and His Spouse the Church (Abbott, *op. cit.*, p. 74).

Therefore, there is a close connection between baptismal grace and religious consecration. The baptismal grace is described in a striking way by St. Paul through the themes of death and resurrection:

> You have been taught that when we were baptized in Christ Jesus we were baptized in his death; in other words, when we were baptized we went into the tomb with him and joined him in death, so that as Christ was raised from the dead by the Father's glory, we too might live a

new life. If in union with Christ we have imitated his death, we shall also imitate him in his resurrection (Rom 6, 3–5).

The baptism of a Christian is the sharing of the agony of Christ's death and of the glory of his resurrection. Every Christian dies and is raised to a new life through baptism. How are the same themes present in the religious consecration: are there aspects of death and life, of agony and glory? Yes, there are. Although no full explanation can be given in short space, the presence of the themes of death and resurrection in the religious consecration can be pointed out.

The foundation of religious vocation is the call to virginity. There, a new life is given: the sharing of the glory of Christ. It is a passage from the power of the *sarx,* body, into the power of the *pneuma,* spirit, in the Pauline sense of the terms. Such a transformation cannot take place without the experience of the Spirit, because without that there would be no attraction to set out on the journey. Conversely, virginity gives a sensitivity and liberates the whole person, mind, heart, and body, for a more abundant reception of God's grace. Since intimate human relations do not capture the attention of the person, the Holy Spirit can hold it continuously. A contemplative grace is always at the origin of virginity, and virginity is the best disposition for the development of contemplative graces. Gradually the whole emotional world of the person can reflect the moods and movements of the Spirit.

In poverty the theme of death is less present; the theme of resurrection is stronger. To be freed from unnecessary involvement with individual creatures, and to take possession of the universe through love and understanding, is probably an anticipation of the world to come.

No one can enjoy this creation so much as the one who discovers God's beauty in it.

Obedience can certainly cause a great deal of agony, and it is not easy to discover the freedom and glory of Christ in it. Such freedom is more frequently asserted than experienced, but it can be experienced. There are, however, some preliminary conditions. It should be understood that obedience means, primarily, dedication to the work of Christ in the visible Church, secondarily, dedication in community. The community aspect should not cloud over the apostolic aspect. Obedience means to free a person for the work of Christ and not to tie him down to little details of daily life which are irrelevant for the work —and for Christ. To continue the redeeming work of Christ can be, and is, exhilarating, but sometimes the power to govern is not used to free the person for the apostolate but rather to imprison him in that earthly solicitude about daily necessities and observances against which our Lord so consistently warned his disciples. No wonder such captive souls can never understand the liberating force of obedience.

Moreover, dedication in community to the work of the Church means an understanding love for the Church, a love that knows fully both the divine and human qualities in the Church. Obedience springs from faith and love: from faith, since it supposes a belief in the presence of a divine mystery behind the Church's human face; from love, since the dedicated person wants to help the Church, and the more the Church appears poor and in need of help, the more tenderly he loves it; such faith and love can be experienced. Sometimes one hears that there is no foundation in the New Testament for religious obedience. The foundation is in the existence of the group of twelve who followed Christ, in their dedication in community (they formed a *collegium*) to the continuation of the work of Christ. One aspect of this community life is precisely obedience; no organic community can exist without some structure that implies an authority to be obeyed by the members. Then, through their obedience, they experience the *kenosis,* the emptying out of their person to the will of the Father. Yet, this emptying out is the path to the most rewarding joys of the apostolate—to the kingdom of God here on the earth.

Just as the life of the Christian can be, and has to be, described as the re-living of the agony of Christ's death and of the joy of his resurrection, so does the life of the religious. Any other presentation of religious life, or of Christian life, would be simply unfaithful to the teaching of the Scriptures. Obviously, the themes of death and resurrection are not just theological terms, but they are living realities that penetrate into the mind and the heart of man. We speak about real agony, as we speak about real joy; every Christian has to live through them and experience them. For consecrated persons death and resurrection cover the specific field of their consecration. Their experience, too, will be specific: they will experience death and resurrection in living their consecration. In them there will be a continuous process of losing their life and finding it.

In Christ's own life, the two periods of death and life were distinct in time. In the case of a Christian and of a religious, they exist enduringly side by side. Through the Spirit whom we receive, eternity is in us, we are redeemed. At the same time, we still have to go through the death of Christ. No other presentation of religious life would be faithful to our Christian tradition. We here touch one of

the basic facts of Christian life: we have to be transformed
from darkness into light, from flesh into spirit. These biblical words indicate the process of transformation going on
in every person who is called to die and to live again.

The process of a Christian growing into the adulthood of
Christ can be analyzed in different ways. I shall try to
point out some important aspects of it, especially those
that have greater importance in the development of contemplative life in religious persons and communities.

The initiative in this pilgrim's progress towards God
lies with the Holy Spirit. He calls a man, he gives him
light and strength all the way. I am more concerned here,
however, with the human response, or with the wisdom
that should fill the mind and the heart of a child of God in
his dynamic relationship with the Holy Spirit.

We read in the Epistle to the Hebrews:

> At various times in the past and in various different ways,
> God spoke to our ancestors through the prophets; but in
> our own time, the last days, he has spoken to us through
> his Son, the Son that he has appointed to inherit every-
> thing and through whom he made everything there is. He
> is the radiant light of God's glory and the perfect copy of
> his nature, sustaining the universe by his powerful com-
> mand; and now that he has destroyed the defilement of
> sin, he has gone to take his place in heaven at the right
> hand of divine Majesty (Heb 1, 1–3).

Our first duty is to listen to God who speaks his word
to us through the inspired text of the Scripture, and
through the Church. We have to read the word of God with
the same insight that the Church has, and with insight simi-

lar to that of the great Doctors of the Church. We have to read the Scriptures with the same mind with which they have been read all through the centuries in order to get a sense of the continuity of the living word of God in the Church. The "same mind" does not mean the same interpretation in all details. The reading of the Bible is an art to be learned at the school of the Holy Spirit and of the great Christian writers, and at the modern schools of biblical sciences. The Bible has to be read together with Christian classics. To mention only a few names, St. Ignatius of Antioch, St. Augustine, St. Gregory the Great, St. Bernard and, in more recent times, St. Teresa and St. John of the Cross are all interpreters of the word in the holiest sense of the term. They bring us this living word of God, provided we are able to understand their books in the right way.

In most spiritual writers three levels of communication can be distinguished. Some of their writings refer to their own strictly personal relationship with God which is unique and cannot be imitated or reproduced by anyone else. Some of what they say was intended for their own time, or for their own religious institute. Finally, there is always in their books a plain Catholic core that is for all persons, all seasons, and all ages. Once we get to this third depth, to the substantial core, we can find in all such works a harmonious stream of thought that enriches everyone from apostolic times to this very day. The differences between the substance of doctrine in the spiritual theology of St. Augustine, St. Gregory the Great, St. Bernard, the author of the *Imitation of Christ,* St. Ignatius of Loyola and, let us say, Charles de Foucauld, will not be great. Once the doctrine is freed from accessories, we find something of the eternal message of Christ. But it takes a discerning and grown-up Christian to read in this way. Children will put down a whole volume if they do not like a line in it; they will not even realize what they are missing.

While the sense of continuity is essential, the finding of new insights through modern writers is also essential, because it is there that we can add to the past inspirations of the Holy Spirit the new ones that are intended for our own age.

The knowledge of God should develop through such reflective reading of his word. The understanding of the word of God will be helped by the Holy Spirit who is present in the word, and in the person who hears it. The more one progresses, the more this internal light from the Holy Spirit grows and the more the word of God comes alive. This "divine reading," as it was traditionally called, remains always the best type of meditation: through it the word penetrates the heart like a two-edged sword. Yet, it should be made clear that the aim and purpose of this reading is to lead us to a Person. However divine the words of Scripture are, they are not God himself but a message from him, and the purpose of the message is to put us into personal contact with God. As this personal contact cannot come into being without receiving the word, so it cannot be kept alive without being nourished by the word. It cannot even be expressed without the use of the word; yet, the word exists for the sake of this personal union.

Religious institutes, working on the renewal of their way of life, should give ample time to their members for this reflective reading of the word of God. The beginning of all wisdom is there. To omit this "divine reading," or to restrict it, as is sometimes done, to fifteen minutes a day and no more, is to block the flow of living waters into the life of the community. Especially in those institutes that devote themselves to external apostolic work, this meditative or contemplative reading has primary importance—much greater perhaps than it would have in a monastery.

OPEN TO THE SPIRIT: PERSONAL PRAYER

The personal relationship between God and a consecrated person requires mutual personal communication. God wants to converse with his friend; man needs a living contact with God. Such personal communication is frequently called the private prayer of religious. The term is misleading: all prayer of a religious is public prayer since his consecration is public. Through this consecration he takes up a new position in the visible Church and all his acts become an act of public cult and worship. He always prays in the name of the whole Christian community, even when he is seemingly praying alone. There should be no exaggerated emphasis on common prayer. We need both personal prayer and prayer in community: wisdom lies in blending the two into a harmonious one and not in abandoning either. Religious are persons in community.

The problem of personal prayer is frequently discussed in reference to man alone. The question is posed whether or not one needs such prayer, or profits from it. The real question, however, is whether or not God wants such personal communication. If he does, we have to respect his desire and take up the thread of conversation. The evidence that God wants to speak to man in a personal way is overwhelming: ever since he called Abraham he spoke in a personal way to every one of the prophets, to most of them in the desert—or in some sort of solitude.

A consecrated person will not be able to be open to the Spirit and to fulfill his prophetic vocation unless he is

in personal contact with God. Ordinarily this demands
some silence and solitude. The capacities of our human
nature are limited: we cannot carry on a conversation with
several persons simultaneously. Anyone who wants to
communicate personally with God will have to direct his
attentions to the Holy Spirit living in him. But the inspirations of the Spirit are always gentle and subtle; they
require our *full* attention. Hence external noise should be
excluded, internal worries should be calmed. When there
is peace, the voice of the Spirit will be heard. It follows
that time, physical time, is necessary to meet God in
prayer. All methods of prayer are good and useful so long
as they warm our humanity to the invisible action of the
Holy Spirit.

The annual retreat of religious should be a time to
enjoy the freedom and hospitality of the Spirit. Unfortunately, in many cases and places it becomes a summer
school of spirituality, useful in itself, perhaps, but leaving
many religious frustrated and cold. No wonder: unconsciously they were anticipating meeting a Person, and they
were fed with ideas about the same Person. When one is
looking forward to meeting a friend and encounters others, who, although they give long lectures on the greatness
of friendship, or even on the person of the friend, do not
allow any personal encounter to take place, disappointment and frustration are inevitable. Many retreats in religious houses are rather an impediment to personal friendship with God than a happy occasion for the meeting of
friends. Quite obviously, graces given during the retreat
should be communicated to others, in the form of dialog,
but this is probably best done after and not during the
retreat. The Holy Spirit has his own exigencies: he is the
jealous God of Israel. Being a Person, he too wants some

time reserved for personal communication with his friends.

In general, such personal communications are warranted by the apostolic aspects of religious life. To be an apostle is to be a messenger. Now, no one can deliver a message unless he has received it from another person. Without personal prayer a deeply apostolic life simply cannot develop, because no one can be a witness to Christ unless he knows Christ personally. It is also difficult to conceive how religious consecration can be kept alive without personal prayer. Virginity is a burden unless the experience of a Person present fills the heart. If there is no personal prayer, there will be an emptiness—and to live in emptiness is neither human nor Christian. Moreover, in personal prayer we are able to penetrate behind the surface of created things and perceive God's immense beauty in them. Finally, it is the human face of the Church that we continually see and experience, and we could easily stop there unless we are in living, refreshing relationship with the Spirit of God who gives life to the Church.

OPEN TO THE SPIRIT: ACCEPTING HIS GIFTS

Union with God is a dynamic gift: God takes the initiative and man receives it. However, it is important to note that in this process God and man play slightly different roles from beginning to end. God will appear increasingly active; man will therefore become increasingly receptive. In the beginning, God communicates himself strongly (but not exclusively) through created objects and images; later he seeks a closer relationship from Person to person without created media. God always takes the initiative; yet, man can somehow use the grace received to dispose himself for the next gift. Reflective reading of the Scriptures, meditation on the word of God can be described as an active warming-up process for the reception of the gift of the Holy Spirit. This entails a human effort: man prepares his mind for the inspiration of the Spirit by using concepts, images, and his reasoning faculties.

There comes a time, however, when God himself wants to talk to men as from Person to person without much use of concepts and images. Then he infuses, more intensely than ever before, grace in the form of light and of love: the recipient feels blinded.

No writer described this transformation with such classic, and even poetic, beauty as St. John of the Cross. His doctrinal exposé becomes even more transparent if it is considered apart from the description of his personal graces, or from the references to his Carmelite charism. Then it all appears in a simpler Catholic splendor, and it states that the transformation of man into God, or our growing up into the adulthood of Christians, takes place through faith, hope, and charity. The progress takes on a rapid rate of growth when God becomes more active and man more passive, when the Good Sheperd begins to lead the sheep. In theory, we may not understand much of this process, but on a practical level, it is important that when God works on the individual's mind and heart, the person should not disturb this work, but should know how to remain passive under the impact of grace. This passivity is, of course, the passivity of the flour that receives the yeast which will transform the lump of dough into fresh and tasty bread that will nourish a man's life. Anyone thus transformed will be, in due course, more active in the service of the Church than he could have been without this transformation.

It is proper to mention here that the graces God offers to different persons are adapted to the way of life to which God called the same person; one gift follows the other in unity and harmony. For those who live in monasteries or enclosed convents, God's graces will be more in the form of light; light to the mind by way of wisdom and understanding. The fruit of the Spirit in their lives may yield some excellent teaching for the whole Church. This was the case of a St. Bernard, a St. Teresa, or a St. John of the Cross. For those who have been called to follow the apostles' way of life, that is, dedication to the external works of apostolate, God's grace may consist in an intense communication of strength. The full maturity of such a gift will lie in the sacrifice of the person's life, either by consuming work for the kingdom, or, rarely, by physical martyrdom. A comparison will illustrate this thought. God gave intellectual graces to St. Teresa, and many in the Church are inspired by her spirited description of the Seven Mansions of the Interior Castle, the Castle of the Soul. God did not give the same insight into the working of his grace, or the same gift of expression to a St. John de Brébeuf; God gave him the strength to accept peacefully all the tortures the Iroquois Indians could inflict on him. St. Teresa had ecstatic visions; St. John de Brébeuf died in what could be called an ecstasy of charity. She received the communication of divine wisdom; he received the communication of divine strength, but both of them reached the maturity of union with God. Both were pure of heart, both were united to God. We come back to the same thought: God deals with each one as a person, and there is no general rule valid for all, except one: we should receive his personal graces intended for us and use them here and now as fully as we can. Some of us may end our life on earth in peace and joy; some of us may go through the agony of Christ in dying. The difference will be accidental. What matters is that in life and death we should adhere to God in mind and heart.

Once this deep and personal impact of the Holy Spirit on a person develops either in the form of communication of wisdom, or in the form of communication of strength, such a person is bound by no law, for he is led by the Spirit of God. This does not mean that the one led by the Spirit is dispensed from the laws of the Church or from the rules of his institute; it means only that within the framework of these laws and these constitutions, God is personally leading and helping the Church through the individual, who will lead many others to the kingdom.

LITURGICAL PRAYER: LITURGICAL ACTION

The importance of the liturgy has been stated by the Council; we read in the Constitution on the Sacred Liturgy:

> For it is through the liturgy, especially the divine Eucharistic Sacrifice, that "the work of our redemption is exercised." The liturgy is thus the outstanding means by which the faithful can express in their lives, and manifest to others, the mystery of Christ and the real nature of the true Church (Abbott, *op. cit.*, p. 137).

This is not the place to give a detailed explanation of the liturgical life of a religious person or of a religious community. It should be done at much greater length than I am able to devote to it in this book. Some great principles should nevertheless be recalled because of their importance for the building up of the contemplative life of a religious institute.

The work of our redemption is exercised and completed by the servant of Yahweh, Jesus, who is the Christ, the Messiah. We are redeemed by his death and resurrection; both the death and the resurrection of Christ are present in the life of the Church: in it the work of the redemption and sanctification of the world continues until the end of time. Through the sacraments, Christ living, in the Church meets his people and justifies, purifies, and sanctifies them. Liturgy means the prayer and the action of the living Christ on earth. Among the sacraments, the Eucharist stands at the center as the source and the consummation of all graces.

It is self-evident that the celebration of the eucharistic sacrifice should be the source and center of the life of the community. It is there that the members become *one* in receiving the undivided body and blood of Christ, and by sharing his immortality. They receive Christ, or better, they are received by Christ. They share his eternal life, they enter the kingdom.

There is a real problem with the sacrament of penance, a problem that stems from the fact that the two aspects of the sacrament are not clearly distinguished: the aspect of reconciliation for those who have broken their communion with the Church, and the aspect of purification for those who are in communion, but seek deeper sanctification. In ordinary circumstances when there is a serious break, reconciliation is not possible without confessing the grave fault. But if there is no definitive break, it is enough for those who are in union with Christ to point to their own sinful humanity in order to obtain his purifying grace.

If there is no need for reconciliation because the union was never broken, the sacrament of penance works

as a healing and purifying gesture of Christ; its repetition
is the extension of Christ's blessing, as the repeated reception of the Eucharist is the deepening of eternal life in us.
Unfortunately, in the past the emphasis has frequently
been put on the wrong element in the sacrament, namely,
on the enumeration of sins. The list of sins has its importance when someone asks for reconciliation after a breach,
but not when someone asks for a deeper union through
greater purity of heart. The sacrament of penance comes
into being when the contrite heart of the faithful and the
healing gesture of Christ in the absolution are joined together.

When there is a rupture in the communion of faith
or charity with the Church, it is necessary to tell the
Church about the break by confessing the sin. When there
is no rupture it is enough to tell the Church that a contrite heart begs to receive Christ's grace. To bring up continually from the past long forgotten and forgiven sins is
rather a demonstration of a lack of trust in the saving
power of Christ than a sign of true contrition. There is
no evidence from the history of the sacrament that so-
called "matter" in the form of sins is required when there
is no grave sin to confess; then the matter is simply our
sinful humanity—without any specification. The sacrament
of penance is a meeting with Christ to receive his sanctifying power. Such an encounter can probably be celebrated in common, provided there is ample opportunity
offered for personal meeting with the priest. Conceived
and celebrated in this way, the sacrament of penance can
be one of the major events in the life of a religious community. Through the absolution coming from the mystical
Christ, the Church, the community is prepared and puri-

fied for the eucharistic sacrifice; such preparation will be needed with some frequency.

Obviously, the present legislation about the confession of religious will be subject to evolution, but the real progress should come, not from the laws, but from the deeper understanding of the action of Christ in the sacrament.

Other liturgical celebrations, such as the saying or the singing of the divine office or common prayers, should, according to the mind of the Church, be inserted into the liturgical activity of the community taken in a much broader sense. By liturgy, we can mean the public worship of the Church, but we should mean also, and in a fuller and deeper sense, the prayers and the actions of publicly consecrated persons. Now, religious persons are holy because they are publicly consecrated, and if they truly live their consecration, the strength of God is in them. It follows that all their prayers and all their actions participate in the public nature of their consecration. In a true sense the care of the sick in a hospital by a consecrated religious is a liturgical action, and his rounds, although they may betray signs of weariness and distraction, partake of the public liturgical cult of God in the Church. In a similar way, a consecrated teacher in a classroom performs a liturgical activity. He announces the good news of the Gospel—and not only when he teaches specifically religious subjects—and therefore his actions are part of the public worship of the Church. Nothing can substitute for participation in the eucharistic sacrifice, or for the reception of the sacraments; but participation in the other prayers of the Church should be balanced against this public cult in the service of the members of Christ.

An enclosed community not dedicated to external apostolic work should take a full share in the celebration of traditional liturgical prayer, in saying or chanting the office. A community dedicated to external apostolic work should have its source of life in the Eucharist, its source of purity of heart in the sacrament of penance, but it should not conceive that it leads a stunted liturgical life because it is devoted to the care of the poor and the ignorant and does not say the divine office.

This is not to say that communities should not pray together—they should. It belongs to the essence of community life that members should be united in the praise of God. It is to say, however, that there should be a balance between the cult of God through apostolic action and the cult of God through his praise in the Church—not all are called to do both. Most religious are called to do one or the other; but all are called to take part in what has been called "cosmic liturgy," the work of redemption in the simplicity of the acts of Christ and of the apostles themselves. This is to share, somehow, in the redeeming activity of Christ in its simple beauty, its divine strength and its ordinary human form.

CONCLUSION

The aim of all consecrated persons and of their communities should be not so much to reach perfection or to lead a perfect life, as to keep in continuous contact with the living Spirit of God. He will lead them and teach them to fulfill his will according to their capacity at a given moment. Such an outlook can relieve a great deal of tension; it can also put an end to so much disappointment that exists among religious who feel that they are not able to achieve perfection.

Moreover, religious persons and communities should be careful not to think of the great God as a small-minded person. God is mainly interested in the personal devotion and loyalty of each one. This loyalty is best shown through our living faith, hope, and charity; all other virtues are of secondary importance. God is like a good father—more than once he finds reasons for joy even in the mistakes and in the very earthly character of his children. Our Lord was careful to instill faith into Peter, to strengthen him in his trust, and to lead him to great love, but he was not over-concerned about Peter's impetuosity, which would probably be described by many as an imperfection. This reflection in no way belittles the so-called small virtues, but it certainly is a plea that proportion should be observed: great virtues should be called great and small ones small. God loves reality.

The contemplative aspects of religious life should penetrate into the life of the community and each one of its members. The order of the day in the community should reflect a certain peace in which there can be openness to the inspirations of the Holy Spirit. There should be periods of silence in the community, or places in the house where the inspirations of the Holy Spirit can be perceived; at the same time, the whole community should participate in that powerful movement that the presence of the Holy Spirit implies, and in the fire that he brings on the earth. Contemplation in this sense is simply essential for religious life, since it is the life of the prophets of the New Covenant. To be a prophet means to be in touch with God—to receive his message, and to obtain strength to carry out his mandate. To be a prophet means, as well, to carry the needs of people to God. It is definitely a personal vocation, but it has to be fulfilled in a community, and, therefore, the life of the community too has to be open to the Spirit. The daily order, the external structures, the text of the constitutions, all should be conceived in such a way that there is in them an opening to the quiet flow of contemplation. The living bond between God and his prophets is established and kept alive precisely by this mysterious communication. Contemplation in this sense is essential for both the person and the community. If there is no communication between them and God, personally and in community, there is no openness to God, and consequently no possibility of carrying God's message.

In this context, only, can we understand why the Council states that all religious must be contemplative; they must adhere to God in their mind and heart. This explains also why it is meaningless to set up hierarchies between various types of religious life. It is the mystery of God's will why he leads some into a solitary place to pray for his people, and why he leads others to minister in a busy place. Both ways of being a prophet come from the same source, their value is the same, that of a divine mandate. It is Christ who gives life through his Spirit to his servants, the ministers of the New Covenant.

8

Love of the World: Apostolic Action

If anyone had asked an Israelite, at any time during the Old Alliance of God with his people, if his God was contemplation or action, the man probably would not have understood the question. He would have wondered what it meant; and then, perhaps, he would have answered by saying: "Yahweh, our God, has spoken to his people, he saved his people from the captivity of Egypt, he is speaking to his people through the prophets, and he is protecting us through his mighty deeds." In other terms, the image that the Israelites had of their God—of this true God—was that of a God eternally active on behalf of his people.

There is no doubt that the image of God that arises from the Bible is the image of a Person who speaks and works to help and to save his chosen people. The Bible story begins with the mighty deeds of God in the creation of the world, and the history of the Israelites is a recounting of, and the reflection on, God's practical love for his people. When the fullness of time came, then the glory of God was manifested in a dynamic way by the life, passion, and resurrection of Christ.

The beginning of the history of the Church is all movement. When the Holy Spirit was given to the apostles, there was a strong wind that shook the house, and tongues of fire appeared over the head of each one to signify in a visible way the invisible presence of God. The life of the Church, too, is marked by divine action. The word of God is being spread from one end of the earth to the other, and the whole creation is being sanctified by the sacraments, the mighty deeds of Christ through the Church.

As Christians reflected on the mystery of an eternally active God, they found its source in the life of the Holy Trinity. There is, to be sure, eternal contemplation among the divine Persons, but there is also eternal action. The Son is being born from the Father, and the Holy Spirit proceeds from the Father and from the Son. Life itself, at the very highest level, means both rest and action. It is difficult for us to realize the unity of these two opposing principles. We are inclined to separate contemplation from action, but in the life of God the two are one. No reasoning can penetrate this mystery, but a Christian intuition can sense something of it.

Even when God revealed himself in his creation, we find that he implanted in all beings both a principle of rest and permanency, and a principle of motion—an imitation of the eternal life of the Trinity, and a splendid revelation to us of God's own life. If this is true of nature, it is even more true of the world of men. Man is the image of God and a Christian is an immortal child of God; accordingly, in the world of men and, even more, in the world of the adopted children of God, we find this revelation of both an eternally contemplative and fully active God.

Religious life is the fruit of the dynamic action of the Holy Spirit in the Church. It can be expected that God will remain faithful to himself and will reveal himself under the twofold aspect of stability and creative action. In him, as from a peaceful source, flows the action that redeems and sanctifies the world; in religious communities, too, there should be a peaceful source from which action flows.

In fact, the Council asserted that all religious institutes are called to both—to contemplation and to apostolic action. Contemplation was considered in the previous chapter. Apostolic action will be the concern of our present reflections.

The best approach is to begin the exposition with the text of the Council:

> To this end, as they seek God before all things and only Him, the members of each community should combine contemplation with apostolic love. By the former they adhere to God in mind and heart; by the latter they strive to associate themselves with the work of redemption and to spread the Kingdom of God (Abbott, *op. cit.*, p. 470).

The immediate conclusion that arises from the text is that just as all religious institutes are called to be contemplative, so all such institutes are called to be apostolic. As it would be wrong to say that some religious institutes are called to contemplation and some are not, so it would be wrong to say that some religious institutes received an apostolic mission while others did not. All are called "to associate themselves with the work of redemption and to spread the Kingdom of God."

In order to acquire a deeper understanding of our apostolic mission, let us go to the Bible for inspiration.

BIBLICAL BACKGROUND

The intention here is not to make an exhaustive research into the meaning of apostolic calling, but rather to take up some themes from the Bible which can help us to gain a deeper understanding of the apostolic aspects of religious life. The themes will be three: prophecy, witnessing, and being sent on a mission. To know what it meant in the Old Testament to be a prophet; what it meant in the New Testament to be a witness of Christ's words and deeds; and finally, what it meant to receive a mission or a commission from Christ, will greatly help us to understand our own apostolic vocation. Obviously enough, there cannot always be a full identity between the gifts of the prophets and apostles and our own gifts, but neither can there be a complete diversity. Much of what we find in the Bible is valid for us too. After all, our own vocation is no less the fruit of God's mighty action than the historical events described in the sacred books.

Prophetic Vocation.   The principal title of a prophet in the Old Testament was that of being a man of God. This was so from the earliest times. When a servant of Saul wanted to lead his master to Samuel, the prophet, he said: "Look, there is a man of God in this town, a man held in honour . . ." (1 Sam 9, 6). The woman of Shunem, who asked her husband to build a small room on the roof for the prophet, Elisha, called the prophet a holy man of God. They were men of God because the spirit of Yahweh possessed them, and they were changed into other men (see 1 Sam 10, 6). This common experience of the prophets of the Old Testament is expressed by Amos:

No more does the Lord Yahweh do anything without revealing his plans to his servants the prophets. The lion roars: who can help feeling afraid? The Lord Yahweh speaks: who can refuse to prophesy? (Am 3, 7–8).

And when a priest, not liking the appearance of Amos, wanted to send him back to guard his flock, the prophet resisted and answered:

> Amos replied to Amaziah 'I was a shepherd, and looked after sycamores: but it was Yahweh who took me from herding the flock, and Yahweh who said, "Go, prophesy to my people Israel"' (Am 7, 14–15).

Since the origin of all true prophecy is the spirit of Yahweh, Israel could not give a prophet to itself; it could elect a king but not a prophet. It was the prerogative of their God to send a prophet. In the Book of Deuteronomy, Yahweh himself makes this clear:

> I will raise up a prophet like yourself for them from their own brothers; I will put my words into his mouth and he shall tell them all I command him. The man who does not listen to my words that he speaks in my name, shall be held answerable to me for it. But the prophet who presumes to say in my name a thing I have not commanded him to say, or who speaks in the name of other gods, that prophet shall die (Dt 18, 18–20).

The very existence of a prophet among God's people is a free gift from God, whose hand cannot be forced. Israel felt this very much during the period when there were no prophets in the land:

> Determined to destroy us once and for all, they burned down every shrine of God in the country. Deprived of signs, with no prophets left, who can say how long this will last? (Ps 74, 8–9)

The prophet is constituted in his vocation by a divine calling.

Moses received his call: "The angel of Yahweh appeared to him in the shape of a flame of fire coming from the middle of a bush" (Ex 3, 2). Moses was sent to Pharaoh to bring the sons of Israel, God's people, out of Egypt.

The boy Samuel heard the call of God while he was ministering to Yahweh in the presence of Eli in the sanctuary where the ark of God was. He was commissioned by God to bring a message of condemnation to Eli and his house. This vocation was never revoked:

> Samuel grew up and Yahweh was with him and let no word of his fall to the ground. All Israel from Dan to Beersheba came to know that Samuel was accredited as a prophet of Yahweh. Yahweh continued to appear in Shiloh, for he revealed himself to Samuel, and the word of Samuel went out to all Israel (1 Sam 3, 19–4, 1).

It is well known how God purified the lips of Isaiah before giving him the mission to be the prophet for the chosen people:

> Then one of the seraphs flew to me, holding in his hand a live coal which he had taken from the altar with a pair of tongs. With this he touched my mouth and said:
> 'See now, this has touched your lips,
> your sin is taken away,
> your iniquity is purged.'
> Then I heard the voice of the Lord saying:
> 'Whom shall I send? Who will be our messenger?'
> I answered, 'Here I am, send me.' He said:
> 'Go, and say to this people,
> "Hear and hear again, but do not understand;
> see and see again, but do not perceive."
> Make the heart of this people gross,
> its ears dull;

shut its eyes,
so that it will not see with its eyes,
hear with its ears,
understand with its heart,
and be converted and healed' (Is 6, 6–10).

While Isaiah offered himself to be a prophet, Jeremiah did not do so. In fact, he accepted his mission reluctantly, and there were days in his life when he regretted that he was ever chosen. The call of Jeremiah is described in the beginning of his book:

The word of Yahweh was addressed to me, saying:
'Before I formed you in the womb I knew you;
before you came to birth I consecrated you;
I have appointed you as prophet to the nations'
I said, 'Ah, Lord Yahweh; look, I do not know how to speak: I am a child!'
But Yahweh replied,
'Do not say, "I am a child."
Go now to those to whom I send you
and say whatever I command you.
Do not be afraid of them,
for I am with you to protect you—
it is Yahweh who speaks!'
Then Yahweh put out his hand and touched my mouth and said to me:
'There! I am putting my words into your mouth.
Look, today I am setting you
over nations and over kingdoms,
to tear up and to knock down,
to destroy and to overthrow,
to build and to plant' (Jer 1, 4–10).

Many other instances could be quoted from the Old Testament, demonstrating this divine initiative by which Yahweh chooses a person to be a man of God, to be an instrument in transmitting his word to the people. In fact, all the previous quotations show that every vocation includes a mission: the prophet receives the word of God, not in order to hide it in his mind and heart, or to speak it within the precincts of his own house, but, symbolically speaking, to go on the rooftops and to announce the message of Yahweh to the whole people of Israel.

In many of the prophets, the word of God receives a new dimension: it is translated into symbolic and highly significant action. Jeremiah bought a field in order to prove his confidence in the future prosperity of Juda. The family life, itself, of Hosea and Isaiah became part of their prophecy. Their marriages, and the children they gave life to, became signs for the whole people. The word of God was not in the prophets' mouths only, but it was translated into action in their lives—in the lives of their families.

The aim of this recollection of the theme of prophecy is not, as has been said, to make an exhaustive research, but to find a source of inspiration for religious life as it is today. Recalling the main lines of thought which we followed in reflecting on the theme, we can compare the life of the prophets with religious life.

Certainly, one of the best descriptions of religious is: God's consecrated people informed by the Spirit of God. Every consecrated person, in a symbolic way, entered the house of God because of an overwhelming inspiration of the Spirit. Not everyone reflects on this fact and is able to put it into words; but the undertaking of a life of virginity, poverty, obedience, and apostolic charity, in itself demonstrates the presence of God's dynamic word in a person. All vocations come from God. As in the case of the prophets, so in the case of religious, the divine call means the handing over, the communication of the word of God, of the word that has to come alive in their lives. Many prophets translated the word into symbolic action. Religious receive the word and translate it into a life of virginity, poverty, obedience, and charity. But the word has to be given to God's people; it is substantially a message about the kingdom. To receive the word implies a mission to God's people. This is why all religious institutes have an apostolic vocation. There cannot be any exception. It is the essence of prophetic vocation.

Called to Witness.   The idea of being a witness, and the regulation for taking a testimony, goes back to the earliest times of the history of Israel. Originally, witnessing meant a legal act requiring the testimony of two persons for the credibility of a fact. Later on, the concept received a theological dimension. For instance, King David was called a witness of God's fidelity:

> His dynasty shall last for ever, I see his throne like the sun, enduring for ever like the moon, that faithful witness in the sky (Ps 89, 36–37).

This call to be witness of God was extended to the whole people of Israel:

> With you I will make an everlasting covenant out of the favors promised to David. See, I have made of you a witness to the peoples, a leader and a master of the nations (Is 55, 3–4).

It is from the Old Testament that the rich theological doctrine of witnessing developed in the New Testament. The coming of Christ is described as an act of testimony. He is "the faithful witness, the First-born from the dead, the Ruler of the kings of the earth" (Rev 1, 5). Jesus came to the world to be a witness of the truth:

'So you are a king then?' said Pilate. 'It is you who say it' answered Jesus. 'Yes, I am a king. I was born for this, I came into the world for this: to bear witness to the truth; and all who are on the side of truth listen to my voice' (Jn 18, 37).

Jesus' witnessing for the truth is surrounded by other testimonies which make it even clearer for us. John the Baptist is a witness that Jesus is the Messiah, the Lamb of God who takes away the sins of the world. St. John states that the Father, himself, attested to the divine mission of his Son:

> But my testimony is greater than John's: the works my Father has given me to carry out, these same works of mine testify that the Father has sent me. Besides, the Father who sent me bears witness to me himself (Jn 5, 36–37).

Finally, the Holy Spirit puts the seal of his testimony on Jesus' life, on his passion and his resurrection:

> Jesus Christ who came by water and blood, not with water only, but with water and blood; with the Spirit as another witness—since the Spirit is the truth—so that there are three witnesses, the Spirit, the water and the blood (1 Jn 5, 6–8).

As Christ witnessed to us the saving mystery of the Father, so his apostles will have to be witnesses of Christ's life from his baptism by John until the time he rose into heaven. They have to witness especially his resurrection which established him as the Lord—Master of all men. To be an apostle is synonymous with being a witness of Christ's saving power:

> . . . but you will receive power when the Holy Spirit comes on you, and then you will be my witnesses not only

in Jerusalem but throughout Judaea and Samaria, and indeed to the ends of the earth (Acts 1, 8).

The testimony of the apostles had to refer not only to Jesus' teaching and preaching, to his passion and resurrection, that is, to his visible life among us, but also, with the help of the Holy Spirit, to the invisible mystery—to the divine mystery—behind the historical facts of Christ's life. They had to witness that the Word was made flesh:

> . . . the Word, who is life—this is our subject. That life was made visible: we saw it and we are giving our testimony . . . (1 Jn 1, 1–2).

It is easy to see how closely the call to be a witness of the kingdom of God is related to the call to be a prophet. The two vocations overlap. No one can be a Christian witness who does not have the personal experience of the presence of the Spirit attesting the truth of the Good News. A disciple of Christ is essentially a witness of Christ: he has to transmit his knowledge of the evangelical facts and his experience of the Spirit to others so that the kingdom of God can expand and the Spirit of God can fill the earth. Without this call to be a witness, no one can be a disciple.

The source of religious vocation is an experience of the action of the Holy Spirit in this world. The testimony of the Spirit leads, then, to another experience: to that of an invisible, divine mystery hidden in the visible, human Church of Christ. By accepting the gifts of virginity, poverty, obedience, and charity all religious declare a personal experience of the action of the Spirit. By submitting themselves to the Church, they declare another experience which is the finding of Christ in the Church. Therefore, religious are in a very special position to witness the kingdom of God, and to tell other persons about it. Their witnessing has to be both collective and personal. It has to be collective because their communities have been gathered by the Spirit. It has to be personal because the members joined a community through the personal inspiration of the Spirit and through the superhuman strength they personally received from him.

Both communities and individual members have to remain open to the Spirit. Their initial experience cannot be a passing event but it has to be permanent, it has to be woven into their lives. The receiving of a vocation or the gathering of those who are called into a community is just the beginning of this life in the Spirit. The structure of the life of a community should be such that it is all the time open to the Spirit, and the members are able to experience the kingdom of God so that they can give testimony to the world that God is alive. Their testimony is twofold: they are witnesses of the resurrection and of Christ's continuing life in the Church. No religious community can exist without fulfilling this duty of being a witness.

Perhaps here is the best place to say in what sense religious are a sign of the kingdom of God. They are not an empty sign; they are a sign because there is an incarnation of the kingdom in their lives. They received the specific gifts of virginity, poverty, obedience and apostolic charity; therefore their whole life points toward the kingdom, it leads God's pilgrims to the kingdom. They are a sign because of the special and internal value of their gifts.

Sent by God. When the Church sends a religious to preach the Gospel, to heal the sick, to bless the little ones, it is repeating a gesture that has always been present in the history of our salvation. In the beginning, the people of

Israel were chosen by God to carry the revelation of God to all nations. In this collective mission, given to the whole people, the vocation of the prophets and the testimony of God's witnesses was included. This great mission was revealed first to Abraham: "All the nations of the earth shall bless themselves by your descendants . . ." (Gen 22, 18).

From the time of the exile, Israel became more explicitly aware of this divine mandate. They conceived themselves to be the envoy and the servant of Yahweh: they were Yahweh's messenger. This is the time when the old narrow nationalism was giving place to the consciousness of a universal religious mission.

But there is no more striking declaration of a divine mission than that of our Lord:

> He came to Nazara, where he had been brought up, and went into the synagogue on the sabbath day as he usually did. He stood up to read, and they handed him the scroll of the prophet Isaiah. Unrolling the scroll he found the place where it is written:
>
>> The spirit of the Lord has been given to me,
>> for he has anointed me.
>> He has sent me to bring the good news to the poor,
>> to proclaim liberty to captives
>> and to the blind new sight,
>> to set the downtrodden free,
>> to proclaim the Lord's year of favor (Lk 4, 16–19).

Later in his preaching, our Lord liked to underscore this quality of being an envoy of the Father: *I was sent.* The Son of Man came to announce the Good News, to bring fire on earth, to serve and to give his life for us. All that Christ accomplished had its source in the mission that he received from his Father. The sending of the Son by the Father occupies a central place in the theology of the early

Church. Christ is the Sent One, the *apostolos,* the apostle sent by the Father.

As Christ was sent by his Father, so he sent his own envoys to announce the good news: "And he said to them again, 'Peace be with you. As the Father sent me, so am I sending you'" (Jn 20, 21).

To receive any of these apostles is to receive Christ; to receive Christ is to receive the Father:

> All authority in heaven and on earth has been given to me. Go, therefore, make disciples of all the nations; baptise them in the name of the Father and of the Son and of the Holy Spirit, and teach them to observe all the commands I gave you . . . (Mt 28, 18–20).

Finally, to fulfill this divine mission, the Holy Spirit was given to the apostles and to the disciples. What they could not do by themselves, they were able to do in the Spirit. In him they were clothed with strength; in him they could preach the Good News with power and authority. Through the mystery of baptism and the imposition of their hands, they gave the Spirit to those who believed.

Even after such a short consideration, it is clear how much the apostolic mission is an integral part of consecrated religious vocation. To accept a call to religious life is to accept a mission. This mission is twofold: to announce the word of God and to communicate the strength of God. All religious are called to do this. This duty exists all the time, and it is a duty of the whole community just as much as of the individual persons. In this context of mission it is easier to understand why no religious community could live in good conscience in a building that is not functional and does not reflect an evangelical simplicity. The word of God would not be radiating from the community. It is also because of this mission that the life of the individual religious has to be faithful to the Gospel: he has to proclaim the word of God by his deeds.

Prophecy, witnessing, and mission are three aspects of God's manifestation in this world. The three themes complete and mutually enrich each other. The three together show that no one can be a Christian without being an apostle, and even more, no one can be consecrated to God in a special way without becoming a prophet and a witness sent by God to his people. The consequences for the future development of religious life are probably greater than we can see now. By our whole being we belong to God's people. We have a duty to go to them continuously, uninterruptedly, with the Good News and with the strength of the Spirit. And they have a right to come to us at any time, opportune or inopportune, and ask us about the Messiah. The deeper we reflect on these theological truths, the more we associate ourselves with God who loved this world so much that he sent his only Son into it to redeem it and sanctify it. The whole internal dynamism of religious life points towards God's people who are in need of help and redemption. At the same time, the same Spirit who lives in us inspires those who are seeking Christ to come to the prophets, to the witnesses, and to the messengers—among whom the religious should have an eminent place. God is with his people again.

REFLECTIONS ON REALITY AND TERMINOLOGY

To base these reflections and practical suggestions on solid ground, my own terminology needs clarification. I would like to go to the decree *Perfectae Caritatis* for help, but no doubt the Council itself had difficulties with the use of terms. On the one hand, the Decree says: "The members of each community should combine contemplation with apostolic love" (Abbott, *op. cit.*, p. 470). On the other hand, somewhat later, the text reads: "Members of those communities which are totally dedicated to contemplation . . ." (Abbott, *op. cit.*, p. 471). It is not easy to reconcile these two sentences and to put a full theological meaning on each, unless the terminology of the Council is explained. Really, contemplation cannot be combined with action. Contemplation *is* the source of action, as in ordinary human life, an idea is the source of an action; an idea is not combined with an action. So in the world of grace, contemplation is the infusion of light and strength from which an action is bound to spring. In order to be totally dedicated to Christian action, one has to be totally dedicated to Christian contemplation. There might be degrees in this dedication, but the degree will be the same, whether it is contemplation or action: the two are closely united, they are one, just as the root and the trunk, the branches and the fruit of the tree are one.

It is difficult, therefore, to distinguish communities totally dedicated to contemplation from those not totally dedicated. The difference cannot really lie in contemplation or in a call to union with God; the difference is really in the fruit of the contemplation, in the external way of life, which in one case means an enclosed life with much solitude, silence and penance, in the other case means apostolic action in the world. In due time, though, even a community which remains secluded from the world, but is rooted in the Spirit, will have an impact on the life of the Church and the life of mankind. Such an impact matures slowly and is discovered after reflecting on subtle spiritual forces in history.

It would be absurd to ask which of the two ways of life is more excellent. It would be as absurd as to ask which of the charisms enumerated in the first epistle to the Corinthians is more excellent. They all are given by the Holy Spirit for the building of the Church and each one has its own place. Among them all, charity is the highest charism, and each should strive to be filled with it.

In an attempt to clarify the terminology, one fact can be stated in clear terms: all religious institutes are apostolic. There cannot be any doubt about this statement. It is reasonable, also, to reject the traditional distinction of religious institutes into contemplative, active, and mixed. The arguments against the division are manifold. First, all religious institutes are called to be contemplative. Then, there cannot be true apostolic action in the full sense without its being rooted in the inspiration and strength of the Spirit which is contemplation. Finally, the expression mixed way of life does not make sense. Action has to grow from contemplation; they are organically united, not mixed.

This leaves us with the statement that all institutes should be contemplative and apostolic, and there cannot be mixed institutes. Yet, there is a great difference between the external way of life of various religious communities. How can this difference be described? Here we come to another traditional distinction among the religious institutes, made by the Council itself. It is the distinction between the monastic, conventual, and fully apostolic way of life. The typical representatives of the three different types would be the Benedictines, the Franciscans, and the Jesuits. It is obvious that this distinction cannot be either on the level of contemplation or on the level of apostolic mission, since they all are called to both equally. Therefore, so far as the distinction has a foundation, it must lie in the external way of life of these communities; in the specific approach to the realization of contemplation and action.

To avoid confusion, it might be better to describe this differentiation among religious by speaking about fully enclosed life, moderately enclosed life, and fully open way of life. The Trappists are fully enclosed, dedicated, to a large extent, to traditional monastic observances; the Discalced Carmelite Friars are dedicated to common prayers, penances, and observances, and at the same time they pursue external apostolic activity; they are moderately enclosed. The Jesuits were founded for living and working in the world, and, for practical purposes, they have few common observances. It would be interesting to investigate whether these various types of consecrated life originated in contemporary theology of the spiritual life and how much they owe to the social structures of the time of their foundation. Be that as it may, they all represent a strong tradition in the Church, approved of and proved many times to be eminent instruments of sanctification for the members and for outsiders. The Council wants them all to be preserved. However, when it comes to apostolic work in the Church, they represent different approaches to the problem, and consequently the three must be distinguished. In order to avoid any confusion and also any misunderstanding in my exposition, I shall retain the distinction between the enclosed, semi-enclosed, and openly apostolic way of life. These terms will be further explained as we proceed, but perhaps sufficient clarification has been made. The next task is to say something more about each one of these ways of life.

THE ENCLOSED WAY OF LIFE AND THE APOSTLES' WAY OF LIFE

A terminology is right only when it expresses reality. In the life of the Church, enclosed religious communities are as much a reality as communities open for immediate, apostolic action. Between these two, there are communities that somehow try to share the life of both. It is fitting that under the terminology, reality itself should be described and thus clarified. The best way of doing it is probably to take the two great types of religious life: the one secluded from the world, the other living in the world, and describe them, omitting for the time being the explanation of the type of life which shares the gifts of both, but in itself has no characteristics which would not be found in a stronger form in either of the other two.

It could be said, perhaps, that I am attempting to describe the monastic and the apostolic way of life. I prefer, however, to speak in a concrete way about communities that follow an enclosed way of life and those that follow the apostles' way of life. Let me emphasize that this distinction is in no way a value judgment; all value judgments should be rejected. Let me stress also that the Council again canonized both ways of life: they are both wanted in the Church. It is not my intention, either, to decide which institutes fall into which category. I prefer to remain on the level of facts, and the fact is that there are enclosed communities and there are communities following the apostles' way of life. To be enclosed and not to have immediate contact with the external world is a fact; and to have contact with the external world by the way of life of the apostles, again is a fact. This is something of a phenomenological description of religious life. All are contemplatives but not all contemplatives are secluded; all are apostles but not all apostles follow the apostles' way of life.

The basis for this distinction is that no religious community can reproduce the full life of Christ. Somehow we all follow him partially; therefore there is this division of charisms.

The enclosed communities are called to reproduce primarily, even in an external form, the prayer and the fasting of Christ in the desert. Since they are part of the mystical body of Christ, they hand over the fruit of their solitary friendship with God to communities with external action and to the whole Church and to mankind. Since it is God who calls them to this way of life, he communicates with them, adapting himself with gentleness to their calling and circumstances. The spiritual gifts that God gives to them are usually in the form of light and wisdom; they are gifts for the intellect. The human expression of such graces is in the prayer of praise they offer to God, and in the spiritual instruction they communicate to their fellow men. The divine office developed mainly in monasteries. Some of the best treatises on the spiritual life were written by enclosed monks or nuns.

The way of life of an enclosed community can best be described by saying that it is a continuous effort to create an order from which peace would arise and the lights of the Spirit be better received. The mind has to be kept free for this communication. Therefore an orderly and leisurely rhythm is part of the life of the monastery; leisurely, not in the sense of undue relaxation, but in the sense of keeping the mind free from pressures and from preoccupations. The concept of the Holy Rule plays a large part in establishing these conditions; it is an instrument to keep the whole community as peaceful as possible. In the daily routine of life, uniformity is favored. Whatever disturbs the rhythm of the community life could disturb the members' openness to grace. Common life is of great importance, and a new member is primarily trained to take his place in the community. Accordingly, there is stress on passive obedience and less emphasis on developing creative talents. Not that there is no creativity in such communities; but it is the community rather than the individual members that converts new ideas and ventures into new enterprises.

A community that is open to the world, and externally follows the simple way of life of our Lord in his public ministry, or follows the twelve apostles' way of life, should be no less rooted in God than an enclosed community. Such apostolic communities reproduce, in their life, the teaching, preaching, healing, and blessing work of Christ. God who called these communities into being will communicate his graces to them with respect to their initial gift. He will give them sufficient light for their actions, but his main gift for them will be strength and power for the building of God's kingdom among men. This communication of strength is no less divine than the communication of light, but it is far more difficult to express in human terms. It is always more difficult to comprehend energy than to understand an idea. The apostles' human expression of the graces received will be more in practical actions than in theoretical explanations. The members of the community are more likely to help the Church by their sustained work or, in rare cases, by their martyrdom than by treatises in theology. They rarely will have the opportunity for a common and solemn celebration of the divine office. They please God by their work more than by their words; but their praise is no less valuable for that.

Because of the varying needs of other persons to whom they are sent, their daily routine can hardly be confined to a set pattern. Their openness to the world requires a freedom from undue limitations in time and even in space. Consequently, they will have to rely strongly on the Holy Spirit and on their own creative activity. Their rule of life will not have the absolute character that is so typical of enclosed religious. Most of their rules will serve as guideposts leading towards the kingdom, valid so long as the greater glory of God or the greater good of their fellow men does not postulate that they should ascend higher, from the written rule of man to the unwritten rule of the Holy Spirit. For such a life, a specific training is needed, not so much in strict observance as in a humble, enterprising spirit in Christ.

Perhaps the real theological difference between the two ways of life consists in the different type of mission received from the Church. An enclosed community receives the mission to continue the prayer and the penance of Christ. They formulate a message in the desert to be transmitted to the world by the great means of liturgical prayer and action and perhaps by books. When a person enters into an enclosed community, his primary duty is to accept this mission. He has no vocation to go out of the community; his vocation is to stay in it. A community that follows the apostles' way of life receives a commission from the Church to announce the Gospel to all creatures. The community exists for the sake of other communities: Christ called the apostles for the sake of the Church of Jerusalem, of Corinth, of Rome. The apostles had to found new communities and bring them the gift of Christ. Somewhat summarily, one could say that the person who joins a cloistered community joins it in order to stay with it. A person who joins a community open to the world joins it in order to go out of it to bring the Good News to other communities. They are definitely two different ways of life with two different internal dynamisms that require a different mentality, different inclinations, and above all, a different training—internally and externally—in the young members.

THE FUNDAMENTAL CHOICE

The difference between these two ways of life is so great that, in all probability, every religious institute will be compelled to make a fundamental choice between the two. The temptation to compromise is great, but it seems that such a compromise—at least for practical reasons—becomes increasingly difficult, if not impossible.

The choice is necessary because of the demands of external apostolic action in the modern world. Those who are working in schools, in hospitals, or those who are preaching or are on missionary journeys have to give themselves wholly to their work. When they return to their communities they are in need of refreshment and relaxation. They are not able, physically, psychologically, or even spiritually, to carry out the usual exercises of enclosed religious life. This statement certainly applies to communities living in great cities or in industrial regions; the demands can be somewhat less exacting in the country and in rural places.

The life of an enclosed monk was always a human and balanced way of life. He had plenty of time for quiet reading, he had many hours for praising God, and he had also time for intellectual and physical work. Through the well-regulated rhythm of his daily duties, he found union with

God. It would be a mistake to think that we can do the work of an apostle in the modern world and, at the same time, carry on the observances of all or many monastic practices. There is a limit to what human nature can endure, and no doubt some institutes made the mistake of trying too much. The result was continuous weariness among the members, tensions in the community, lack of capacity to receive the inspirations of the Holy Spirit and to be happy in a human way. From such a state of things a dearth of vocations automatically followed. The only solution lies in healthy humility that admits that the two ways of life cannot be lived together by the same persons or by the same communities.

The choice is postulated also by the difference in the nature of the mission the two types of communities receive from the Church. An enclosed community is called to develop a strong communion among the members through common prayer, common work, and common penances, but they are not called to be in close contact with the community of their fellow men; such contacts will be short and occasional. Therefore, the mind and the heart of the individual will be strongly centered on his own community. Another institute that follows the apostles' way of life receives a mission to go out and to build up a communion with lay members of the Church and with those who, as yet, do not belong to the Church. Every person in the community has to direct his mind and his apostolic desires towards those who are outside the community, not in a way that denies his own community—it will remain a bond of unity, a source of strength—but in a way that is required by the mission given him by the Church. He is sent to all men, as Christ was sent to all men to teach and sanctify them. These two types of orientation cannot easily co-exist in the mind of the same person. He would be easily inclined to follow one and neglect the other or—what would be equally wrong—not to follow wholeheartedly either of the two, but to find a compromise solution that might be halfhearted.

From the different natures of the mission received from the Church, there follows a different way of life in the community. Monks, again in the ancient and classical sense of the term, have to lead a common life. To be fully involved in this common life is the mark and touchstone of the authenticity of the vocation of a monk. Common life means a great deal of uniformity, be it in the schedule, or in sharing the goods of the monastery. Those who follow the apostles' way of life cannot and should not have a common life in this sense. They should form a community, which means that they are one in mind and heart, but does not necessarily mean common exercises throughout the day, or uniformity in the movements of the members present in the house.

Some examples will clarify this observation. Common life requires that the members come together for recreation; to be part of a community requires close contact with the other members of the community, but not necessarily at the same time, since the community is dispersed in apostolic work. Instead of a common time for recreation, perhaps there should be a room where the apostle in need of relaxation can refresh himself by conversing with others. The daily routine should be subject to apostolic needs. In a monastery, all meals should be taken in common. In a community following the apostles' way of life, there should be an opportunity for everyone who is not able to be at home at the time of a meal to obtain or to prepare his own meal.

These external differences have their root in a difference in spirituality. In an enclosed way of life, the spirituality is centered firmly on being an anonymous member of the community. Passive virtues will be stressed: obedience to the Holy Rule, obedience to the abbot; and personal initiative will not be much encouraged. In a community following the apostles' way of life, although passive virtues should be stressed also, since all our actions should be an act of obedience to God, personal initiative and creativity should be steadily and strongly encouraged. In the deepest Christian sense, there should be a cult of community combined and united with a cult of Christian personality.

The training of a young religious in an enclosed community is fully oriented towards making him a good member of that community. The training of a young person who has to follow the apostles' way of life in a community has to be oriented towards working, together with the members of his own community, for other Christian communities. The communitarian aspect in the formation of a young monk will be very different from that in the formation of a young religious preparing to follow the apostles' way of life. Both will have to be good members of their community but in a different way. The monk belongs primarily and constantly to his own community. The religious who follows the apostles' way of life belongs to the community of his fellowmen and of his fellow Christians. In a traditional monastery, personal creativity and enterprising spirit can hardly be encouraged at the expense of the common life. The community will have to be creative and enterprising, but the individual members will have less opportunity for it. In an apostolic community it is essential that, from the very beginning, creativity and personal initiative should be encouraged: creativity that extends over the whole field of Christian life. One can be creative even in the matter of obedience and humility.

Earlier I said that the basic choice between the two ways of life is a practical necessity. I go one step further now to suggest that the choice is a theological necessity. The whole personality of a man cannot be fully dedicated to two contrasting vocations; in these modern times, nothing short of total dedication is sufficient.

Naturally enough, the question arises about those communities described in the Decree on Religious Life as "religious communities which by rule or constitution closely join the apostolic life with choral prayer and monastic observances" (Abbott, *op. cit.*, p. 473). The answer is that probably the Council did not intend to state that this close combination of the two ways of life is always and everywhere possible. I am speaking mainly of situations in big cities and industrial regions. Also, experience seems to show that such communities do, in fact, make the choice very frequently in the direction of the way of life of the apostles. Once the choice is clearly made and a certain outlook and spirituality adopted, there is really not much problem with preserving a few common observances. It is finally a question of a fundamental option and not exactly a choice among various external actions.

A COMMUNITY DEDICATED TO APOSTOLIC ACTION

We could truly say that in an enclosed religious house, there is a community and a common life; but in a religious house dedicated to external apostolic work, there is a community, but little common life. The needs of the body of Christ call members away from common observances. Therefore, it is of great importance that we should try to clarify the meaning of a community in which the members are dedicated to external apostolic action. If they are not held together by a common order of the day, by common prayer and penances, what is it that molds them into one community? Searching for the meaning of a Christian community, we have to return always to the Holy Trinity. It is there that we find a plurality of persons in the oneness of divinity. Community means several persons all sharing what they have with the others. The image of the Trinity should be reflected in every Christian community. Many persons should be one in sharing whatever good things they may possess: the persons remain distinct, their possessions are one. This is what is described in the Acts of the Apostles: "The whole group of believers was united, heart and soul; no one claimed for his own use anything that he had, as everything they owned was held in common" (Acts 4, 32). Even if material things are not possessed in common, there should be a common mind and a common heart which is the primary element in a community.

Christ our Lord stresses that a Christian community is more than the sum of the individuals who happen to be together. He promised that if two or three gather in his name, he will be with them. Therefore a Christian community arises from this presence of Christ.

In a religious community, there are many persons, but there is also a unity. All share gifts: each of them received the same call from God, each of them was accepted in the service of the Church. A religious community is an organ in the mystical body of Christ. Since it is an organ it has an internal finality: it has to serve the whole body. No religious community is an end in itself; it belongs to the Church and it receives the meaning of its existence from this connection with the Church.

The essential elements that make a loose group of Christians into a religious community are the common call and the common charisms they have all received. Behind the community there is the one action of the Holy Spirit, there is the one acceptance from the Church, and it is this spiritual element that makes a group into a community—it is not the common observances but the common grace and the common mission; the common mind, heart, and spirit. Unfortunately, Canon Law still defines religious vocation as life in common; this of course, applies to the enclosed monastic way of life, perhaps to the conventual way of life, but it does not express the vocation of those communities that follow the apostles' way of life. The definition should stress more clearly the common mission received from the Church. Once the spiritual meaning of community is stressed and grasped, it will be easier to order the everyday life of the apostles according to the exigencies of the apostolate.

The way of life that an apostolic community must follow can be described as openness to the Spirit and openness to the world. It must be open to the Spirit since the building of the kingdom is primarily the work of the Spirit. There should therefore be provisions in its constitution to assure that new and unexpected inspirations can be received and put into practice. External apostolic work requires also an openness towards the world and no one should fear that:

> Yes, God loved the world so much that he gave his only Son, so that everyone who believes in him may not be lost but may have eternal life (Jn 3, 16).

As Christ was open to the world, came into this world, the apostle has to go into the world, and he should not be afraid. Christ is with him, he goes with the mission; and Christ has already won his battle with the power of darkness. To be open to the world means to share the dynamic action of God in the incarnation, in the redemption, and in the sanctification of the world.

It is not enough to state the need for this openness only theoretically. It is essential that it be written into the constitutions of religious communities dedicated to the apostles' way of life. It requires a frequent meeting of the legislative authority of the institute—the general chapter—to establish new laws according to the ever changing and increasing needs of the apostolic work. It requires easy and swift administration, the key to which usually lies in decentralization.

The training of young members too has to consist in both the knowledge of God and the knowledge of the world. They are going to be messengers of God; therefore it is indispensable that they should build up a contact with their Master. Their spiritual formation should not be watered down or relaxed; if anything, it should be intensified. No one can be the messenger of another person unless he received a personal message to transmit. At the same time, religious must have a knowledge of the needs of the world. If they do not, much of their work could be irrelevant, even if well meant. The practical consequences can be far reaching. The novitiate should be a school of prayer, but it should not be a schooling in the enclosed way of life. If it is, the first step would be taken in the wrong direction. To achieve the ideal, which is to live and to move in God, novices should have alternate periods of prayer and solitude, and of intense work, so that they may find God in both, but possibly under the guidance of a spiritual director. This alternation of external circumstances would gradually teach them how to deal with difficulties, how to remain united to God in their work, and how to find a unity in their prayer life and apostolic work. A fully monastic novitiate for an institute dedicated to external apostolic work is no less misleading than a mere schoolroom training for a soldier who will have to fight.

The central aim in the training of the young religious should be integration of prayer and work. This is probably the greatest problem for many today. Many have been trained in a secluded novitiate and sent out after such a training to do intense apostolic work; they were not sufficiently, or perhaps not at all, trained to achieve an integration of the two opposite directions in their life. Such a training in integration may require a longer period in the novitiate than is customary now, but if there is no seclusion its prolongation should not cause any practical difficulty. It is fair also to both sides that those who are going to be incorporated into a religious community should be tested in the way of life the institute follows. At present all candidates for the apostles' way of life have to be tested in a novitiate conceived on the pattern of monastic spirituality and observances. No wonder there are many crises of vocation after the novitiate.

Integration between prayer and work is achieved when one learns to discern the work of the Holy Spirit in his own person, in other human beings, and in this created world in general. The Master of our history is God; the good apostle is the one who knows his Master's way of thinking and can sense and follow his actions. Therefore no one can learn how to be an apostle unless he reflects on the action of the Spirit in himself; unless he goes out into the world to meet human persons, to observe the work of the Spirit in them; unless he carefully watches and interprets God's mighty deeds in our turbulent history. Many years are needed to learn such a skill, and it can hardly be done without the help of a guide who has both charity and critical talent.

Should we conclude that our whole conception of the training of young religious should be rethought and the external structures of the training remodeled? No other conclusion is possible. We need new schools where the art of discerning the presence of the Spirit is taught in both theory and practice. They will give us apostles who understand something of the disconcerting wisdom of Christ who wanted to be with his fellow men and redeemed them through his death and resurrection—the mystery of the cross and glory.

Much in the training of those who are called to follow the apostles' way of life will have to be rethought and reformed. No doubt, such a process can be painful, but is not religious life a continuous process of dying and rising from the dead? There is a new Pentecost, and the doors of the house where many fearful disciples prayed are wide open. Those who fear the noise of a powerful wind and see tongues of fire should not hesitate to go out and to shout the Good News. Their risen Master will be with them.